"Jonathan and Shane—along with the many friends they quote and tell stories about in these pages—are on a journey together toward a bold and beautiful way of living that makes people more truly alive. As one trying hard to stay that same course, I am more than grateful to them for sharing in such clear and practical language what they have been learning along the way about prayer, about community, and about keeping faith with God and our brothers and sisters with their backs against the wall."

Bart Campolo, writer, speaker and neighborhood minister

"Not everyone will agree with every particular detail of biblical interpretation in this book by Claiborne and Wilson-Hartgrove, but *no one* can deny the truth of their main argument: God is calling each and all of us to be eager agents fulfilling His purposes in the world! This book compels us passionately to ask, in the power of the Holy Spirit, 'How am I "putting legs on my prayers"?' This is a tested book and a necessary one!"

Marva J. Dawn, teaching fellow in spiritual theology, Regent College, Vancouver, and author of *Unfettered Hope, Joy in Divine Wisdom and My Soul Waits*

"Claiborne and Wilson-Hartgrove have slipped the bonds of the ordinary and leapt the chasm of the customary. They have stood at brightly burning bushes that for most of us just won't catch fire. This book is a small invocation which, once prayed, calls for those who thought they knew the far country to see it for the first time. The far country is not so far as we supposed: it lies vivid and visible betwen our 'our Fathers' and our 'thy will be dones.'"

Calvin Miller, Beeson Divinity School, author of *The Singer* and *The Path of Celtic Prayer*

"God always raises up new and courageous voices when the church is tempted to forget its own gospel. Here are two of those voices—and two who have been made into the answer to our own fervent prayers."

Richard Rohr, O.F.M., Center for Action and Contemplation, Albuquerque, New Mexico

"Who learns more fully about the importance of prayer than folks living in Christian community and engaged in social activism? The authors of this wonderful little book share graciously and truthfully from the spiritual wisdom they have gathered."

Christine D. Pohl, professor of social ethics, Asbury Theological Seminary, and author of *Making Room*

"Jonathan and Shane, contemplative activists, humble prophets, and sincere lovers of humanity and God, provoke a new way of understanding prayer. Avoiding the tendency to reduce prayer to 'three easy steps' or trite formulas, Jonathan and Shane press the integrity of our prayer lives by challenging us to live into our prayerfulness. Rather than suggesting prayer as wishful thinking or hopefulness wrapped around memorized bedtime recitations, *Becoming the Answer to Our Prayers* recovers the essence of truly prayerful life—it's the recovery of a sacrificial embodiment of our prayers. God's answer to our prayers might be as close, or as far away, as our willingness to be available as part of the solution. Jonathan and Shane make this simple truth accessible and available, inspiring us to an authentic prayer life—a life lived to answer prayers."

Christopher L. Heuertz, international director, Word Made Flesh,
and author of *Simple Spirituality: Learning to See God in a Broken World*

Shane Claiborne and
Jonathan Wilson-Hartgrove

BECOMING THE ANSWER TO OUR PRAYERS

PRAYER FOR ORDINARY RADICALS

IVP Books

An imprint of InterVarsity Press
Downers Grove, Illinois

InterVarsity Press
P.O. Box 1400, Downers Grove, IL 60515-1426
World Wide Web: www.ivpress.com
Email: email@ivpress.com

InterVarsity Press® is the book-publishing division of InterVarsity Christian Fellowship/USA®, a student movement active on campus at hundreds of universities, colleges and schools of nursing in the United States of America, and a member movement of the International Fellowship of Evangelical Students. For information about local and regional activities, write Public Relations Dept., InterVarsity Christian Fellowship/USA, 6400 Schroeder Rd., P.O. Box 7895, Madison, WI 53707-7895, or visit the IVCF website at <www.intervarsity.org>.

All Scripture quotations, unless otherwise indicated, are taken from the Holy Bible, Today's New International Version™ Copyright © 2001 by International Bible Society. All rights reserved.

Design: Cindy Kiple
Images: Kamil Vojnar/Getty Images

ISBN 978-0-8308-3622-2

Printed in the United States of America ∞

Library of Congress Cataloging-in-Publication Data

Claiborne, Shane, 1975-
Becoming the answer to our prayers: prayer for ordinary radicals /
Shane Claiborne and Jonathan Wilson-Hartgrove.
    p. cm.
Includes bibliographical references.
ISBN 978-0-8308-3622-2 (pbk.: alk. paper)
1. Bible—Prayers—History and criticism. 2. Prayer—Christianity.
3. Spiritual life. 4. Christian life. 5. Church and social
problems. I. Wilson-Hartgrove, Jonathan, 1980- II. Title.
   BS680.P64C53 2008
   248.3'2—dc22
                          2008022648

P 24 23 22 21 20 19 18 17 16 15 14 13 12 11 10 9 8 7 6 5 4 3 2 1

Y 28 27 26 25 24 23 22 21 20 19 18 17 16 15 14 13 12 11 10 09 08

For our mommas, who keep praying

Contents

Introduction

THIS IS A BOOK ABOUT PRAYER. But it's not really about how to pray. There are lots of good books to help you learn to pray. This one is about becoming the answer to our prayers.

We live in inner-city communities that are usually known for their activism, not their prayer life. In fact, writing this book has been a discipline, as we try to listen amid all the noise of wildly busy lives, and speak nothing more or less than we hear God speaking to us. On good days, it has felt like there were three of us writing together.

We know we need prayer. Like roses need water, we need a connection to God that sustains, guides and makes us into something beautiful. As students at Eastern College, outside of Philadelphia, we fell in love with God's vision for a kingdom on earth where the weak find justice and there are no longer any poor. Learning from friends in the Christian Community Development Association (CCDA), we relocated to neglected neighborhoods and helped start The Simple Way (Philadelphia) and Rutba House (Durham, North Carolina), communities of hospitality and peacemaking. The daily struggle to put our hope in God's light despite the darkness of inner-city blight has driven us to conversation with God. We want to understand prayer because we know we can't live without it.

For many of us who live active lives among the poor and marginalized, prayer doesn't make the top of the urgent to-do list. After all, wouldn't God rather have us feed the masses, help a kid with homework, take a friend to detox, heal the broken or liberate the captive? Surely Amos tells the people of God to shut up with their songs and worship and feasts and festivals, and take care of the poor (Amos 5:21-24). Without justice for the poor, religious activities are little more than annoying noise in the ears of God, and the prayers that used to smell like incense to God become a nauseating stench when there is no flesh bringing those prayers to life.

This is all true. And yet we have seen many a "radical" Christian suffocate, entangled in the weeds of injustice. Even entire "intentional Christian communities" are flailing because they have not learned to pray together. Many of us have a sour taste in our mouths from corny Christian retail, like the signs that say "The family that prays together stays together." We admit that it's often easier to complain (or write a book) than it is to pray. We ourselves confess feeling tired, confused, annoyed, even counterfeit in our prayers.

This is not a book about the kind of prayer where we tell God things God already knows, as if Jesus needs a reminder that kids are dying in Sudan. Nor are we talking about the kind of prayer that excuses us from responsibility. Any time we ask someone for help and hear "I'll pray about that," we know to start working on plan B. As our friend John Perkins from

CCDA says, "When you see someone who needs a handicap ramp, don't go pray for a ramp! Build them a ramp."

When we pray to God asking, "Why don't you do something?" we hear a gentle whisper respond, "I did do something. I made you." Prayer is important. Just as important is the call to become the answer to our prayers.

We have so much to unlearn before we learn.

Our friend Tony Campolo tells the story of his grandson going off to say his evening prayers. The boy said, "Hey everybody, I'm going to pray, does anyone want anything?"

Many of us started off this life praying simple little prayers, trying to ask God to do the things we want. "Take care of Mommy." "Help me not get caught taking cookies." "Help us find our lost puppy." "Help us win the game." No doubt, God has a special ear for the prayers of children, even the silly ones asking for girlfriends and the opportunity to be a cowboy. It's a good thing the Spirit intercedes on our behalf, stepping in to protect us from what we think we want and helping us not to settle for what *we think* we need. It's as if the Spirit says, "Look I know he said he wanted to be a cowboy, but . . ." The longer we pray, the more we are sure of this: *Prayer is not so much about convincing God to do what we want God to do as it is about convincing ourselves to do what God wants us to do.*

Mother Teresa was once asked in an interview, "What do you say when you pray?" She replied, "Nothing, I just listen." So then the reporter asked, "Well then, what does God say to you?" Her answer: "Nothing much, He just listens."

The saints say prayer is less about what we say and more about being with the one we love. Prayer is about having a romance with the Divine. The more deeply we are in love with someone, the less we have to say. In fact, a sure sign that we know someone deeply is the ability to enjoy one another without words—to simply admire each other.

We once heard a wise elder say prayer is like a little girl playing at the feet of her grandma. She doesn't have to say anything or do anything to please her grandma (who is quite content just watching her play). And the most beautiful moment is when the child starts to grow tired. She just crawls into grandma's lap to be rocked, to hear a lullaby, to feel a kiss on the forehead and the warm embrace of love.

We love these images of prayer as a deep and intimate relationship with God. When we sit back and think about prayer in a quiet moment, this is just the sort of experience we long for. But it's hard to remember these images—harder still to imagine what they could look like in the face of urgent needs and tragic loss. It's hard to know what it looks like to be a contemplative in the' hood.

Here's the good news: prayer and action can go together; in fact they must. Otherwise we have little more than a bunch of inactive believers or worn-out activists, and neither do much good for the world. But not all of us are mystics and saints like Francis and Mother Teresa. For some of us, it's hard to know where to begin talking about prayer. So we have turned to Jesus. Beginning with the prayer that Jesus taught his disciples to pray, we ask in part one of this book what it looks like to make the Lord's Prayer a model for daily life. While rooted in the intimacy of children talking to their Father, this prayer is as practical as putting food on the table, paying the bills, getting along with neighbors and wrestling with our egos. As we learn to reimagine the everyday in light of Jesus' prayer, we begin to live in a whole new world.

Part two focuses on Jesus' prayer for the church in John 17. It's one thing to say that prayer invites us into a way of life. But we still have to name the distinctive nature of the way that Jesus walked. If the church is the body of Christ, then we are called to continue in this way. John 17 offers guidance for how we can do that.

But we've already noted the difficulty of making prayer happen. We need something deeper than know-how and practice. We need the spiritual wisdom of those who've walked with Jesus—those who have grown in intimacy with Jesus while becoming the answer to their prayers. In part three we've listened carefully to the wisdom of the saints. We invite you to join us in chasing after Jesus with them.

Thank God, saints were there to teach us the words of prayer before we knew what we were doing. Because the prayers of others are so important, we've scattered some of our favorites on the pages of this book. These prayers are usually more important than what we have to say, so we hope you'll pause to pray these prayers with us.

This book is dedicated to our mommas who've prayed some long nights—and keep praying for us.

Part One

THE LORD'S PRAYER

Our Father in heaven,
hallowed be your name,
your kingdom come,
your will be done,
   on earth as it is in heaven.
Give us today our daily bread.
And forgive us our debts,
   as we also have forgiven our debtors.
And lead us not into temptation,
   but deliver us from the evil one,
for yours is the kingdom
and the power and the glory forever.
Amen.

1

An Invitation to Beloved Community

EVIDENTLY JESUS DIDN'T HAVE A SET CURRICULUM for the 101 course he taught the first disciples. Jesus never said, "Sign up for my course on prayer and I'll teach you how to talk to God." Instead, Jesus announced a new kingdom with words and signs. Despite his lack of a military or political power, Jesus insisted that his ministry was about a new social order that was good news to the poor and downtrodden. To anyone who would listen, Jesus said, "Follow me." Those who did found themselves caught up in an adventure.

Not far into the journey, though, those first disciples realized their need for prayer. Jesus didn't have to tell them. They saw Jesus praying, and they knew they needed some of what he had. "One day Jesus was praying in a certain place. When he finished, one of his disciples said to him, "Lord, teach us to pray" (Luke 11:1).

We feel a little bit like those first disciples. By God's grace, we stumbled into the adventure of God's kingdom and gave our lives to Jesus. We were eager to learn the Scriptures and even more enthusiastic about living them out with our whole lives. Not long into this journey, though, we realized that faithfulness requires something we just don't have on our own. The people who did seem to have it were our elders and mentors who knew how to pray. The disciples' desire was ours, and their question drove us to pay attention to Jesus' response. We started saying the Lord's Prayer every day.

The first word of the Lord's Prayer is *Our*. That's important. The prayer Jesus taught us is a prayer of community and reconciliation, belonging to a new kind of people who have left the land of "me." This new humanity is an exodus people who have entered a promised land of "we," to whom "I" and "mine" and "my" are things of the past. Here our God teaches us the interconnectedness of grace and liberation in a new social order. Here we are judged inasmuch as we judge, and forgiven as we forgive.

The disciples ask Jesus to teach them to pray, and he begins with "Our Father." The Son is calling out to the Father, and the Spirit is interceding for us—a brilliant image of the divine community that declared, "Let us make human beings in our image" (Genesis 1:26). And so we too are made in the image of community. It's our deepest thirst. We are created to love and to be loved. The biblical story begins and ends with community.

When humanity is created, it is not good for one human to be alone, but it is good for humans to help each other. It was community that Jesus taught and lived with his disciples, never sending them out alone. His longest prayer (John 17) is that we would be one as the Father and Son are one. And his promise to us is that the Spirit will be among us, whenever two or three of us gather together. When the Spirit fell upon the early church at Pentecost, there was a divine harmony of foreign tongues and a reconciled community that shared all their possessions in common. The biblical narrative ends with the coming of the New Jerusalem, the City of God, a new heaven and a new earth where all of creation is reconciled, and the lion and the lamb lie down together. Our God is a communal God.

And yet so much in the world tries to rob us of this divine gift, seducing us to settle for independence over interdependence—security over sacrifice—to the point that community looks idealistic and spectacular. We express our deep hunger for belonging through such forms of community as nationalism, biological family, marriage or small group Bible study. And there is some good in all of these. Like appetizers, they give us little glimpses of community. But we often don't make it to the feast. We stop short of the great community that God has invited us into.

ST. PATRICK'S BREASTPLATE

I arise today
Through a mighty strength,
*   the invocation of the Trinity,*
Through the belief in the
*   threeness,*
Through confession of the
*   oneness*
Of the Creator of Creation.

This book is an invitation to join the feast already taking place at the table of our Lord—by becoming the answer to the prayers Scripture teaches us to pray. Jesus established a community in his resurrected body. "This is my body, broken for you" is a physical reminder that we have been baptized into Christ's body. As living members of that body, we speak Christ's words. Praying the Lord's Prayer as members of the church is inviting God to make us what we already are—the beloved community of a new humanity.

Our Father in Heaven

Jesus' prayer does not begin with us or our needs—not even our confessions or our big dreams for the kingdom (though all of these are important and will follow). The prayer begins with a transcendent God beyond the boundaries of this world, whose name is so hallowed that it is not even mentioned. Instead of a name for God, we are given a characteristic of God. God is Father—our Father.[1]

For the young disciples, *father* was a role loaded with meaning—not just a person but a social construct. Fathers were the authorities, the providers and the sustainers of life in a male-dominated culture. But the words Jesus dares to teach us also retain an element of intimacy, love and admiration, especially when Jesus uses the familiar *Abba*. We cannot keep God at a safe distance as "King" or "Lord." The One whose name cannot be spoken is drawing close to us. Jesus dares to call the transcendent one "Papa." What is more, Jesus teaches us to do the same.

There's a beautiful place in the Gospels where Jesus lets the disciples in on a family secret:

> "Truly I tell you," Jesus replied, "no one who has left home
> or brothers or sisters or mother or father or children or

fields for me and the gospel will fail to receive a hundred times as much in this present age: homes, brothers, sisters, mothers, children and fields—along with persecutions—and in the age to come eternal life. But many who are first will be last, and the last first." (Mark 10:29-31)

Jesus assures us that as we leave our possessions and family in allegiance to God's kingdom, we will enter a new household of abundance. But when you look closely, there is a difference between the two nearly identical lists. First, there is an additional "bonus" in the second list—persecutions! Persecutions will come to us when we choose an economic order different from the pattern of the world.

But there is also an omission from the second list—fathers. As we are reborn, we leave our biological families. Now we have sisters and brothers and mothers all over the world. And yet Mark's omission of fathers is very intentional, consistent with Christ's teaching: "do not call anyone on earth 'father,' for you have one Father, and he is in heaven" (Matthew 23:9). In an age when fathers were seen as the lifeline of the family, the seemingly indispensable authority and providential centerpiece, Jesus suggests that we have one Father. Only God is worthy to be seen as Father, the Provider and Authority (and, of course, King).

Here's the incredible clincher in these verses: the multiplication is not just in the age to come—crowns, streets of gold and mansions in heaven. The multiplication of resources begins "in this present age." Jesus had homes everywhere he went. He taught the disciples this reality as he commanded them not to take anything for their journey—no bag, no extra food, no clothes, no money, no shoes. By ordering them not to take their stuff, Jesus was implying that they could have taken it—that some of them had access to those things. The disciples were not sent out in the simple poverty of an ascetic life but with a new vision of interdependence, trusting that God would provide for them. One of the early Christians wrote, "We have no house, but we have homes." As the disciples entered a town, others would open their homes. And if not, they were to shake the dust off their feet and move on. This made clear that the church was not only to practice hospitality, but to be dependent on hospitality also. The line between "us" and "them" was dissolved.

In the beloved community of God's kingdom, we have come to see that the family of our Father is a reality in this world. A married couple in England who were unable to have children happened to meet Jane, who had found herself six months pregnant and homeless. So they invited Jane into their home. It proved to be such a beautiful experience that they decided to continue living together and help raise the new baby girl while Jane pursued her dream of going back to school and becoming a nurse.

Some fifteen years later I (Shane) was able to stay with this family on a visit to England. They were indeed a family. The baby was a teenager, and Jane had become a nurse. The woman who took Jane in was ill with multiple sclerosis. But she had a nurse (Jane) living in her home to care for her just as Jane was once cared for. This is the gift of providence and radical interdependence in the beloved community.

The echoes of Jesus' new vision of family are scattered throughout the Scriptures. When a guy from reputable lineage comes and asks Jesus what he needs to do to enter the kingdom, Jesus tells him he needs to be born again (John 3). When Jesus' own mother and brothers come looking for him, he asks, "who are my mother and brothers, but those who do the will of God?" (see Mark 3:31-35). And of course there's the time Jesus says that unless you "hate" your own family you are not ready to be his disciple (Luke 14:26). Jesus is not shunning love for one's own family; he's redefining the boundaries of that love. You might say that he's expanding "family values." As he is dying on the cross, one of the last

---

Glory to thee, Father. Glory to thee, Word. Glory to thee, Grace. Glory to thee, Spirit. Glory to thee, holy one, Glory to thy glory. We praise thee, Father. We thank thee, O Light in whom there is no darkness. And that for which we give thanks is announced by him: I will be saved, and I will save. I will be loosed, and I will loose. I will be wounded, and I will wound. I will be born, and I will give birth. I will eat, and I will be eaten. I will hear, and I will be heard. I will be thought, being wholly thought. I will be washed, and I will wash. Grace leads the dance, I will make music, you shall all dance in a ring. I will lament, you shall all beat your breasts. I will flee, and I will stay. I will adorn, and I will be adorned. I will be united, and I will unite. I have no house, and I have houses. I have no home, and I have homes. I have no temple, and I have temples. A lamp I am to thee that dost perceive me. A door I am to thee that dost knock at me. A way I am to thee, a traveler. Join thee now unto my dancing.

"Dance Hymn," *Acts of John 94-95*

---

things Jesus does is tell his mother that she has a new son (John), and John that he has a new mother.

In the beloved community of "Our Father," the same desperate love that a mother has for her baby or that a child has for his or her daddy is extended to all our human family. Biological family is too small a vision. Nationalism is far too myopic. A love for our own relatives or the people of our own country is not a bad thing. But our love does not stop at the border. We now have a family that includes but transcends biology and geography. We have family in Iraq, Peru, Afghanistan and Sudan. We have family members who are starving and homeless, dying of AIDS and living in the midst of war. This is the new family of our Father.

Father not only defines our relationship with God in a new way; it also changes our relationships with neighbors. It is a betrayal of the "Our Father" to pray "My Father," for the prayer is not only a declaration of a heavenly parent, but it is a commitment to a new vision of family rooted in the providence and authority of our heavenly parent. We cannot have God as Father if we deny the sisterhood and brotherhood we share with the rest of God's children.

This is the point where our rebirth begins to mess with us. For the church as we know it is a tragically dysfunctional family, in which some children are starving while others have food stashed in their closets. Some of us are living on the street while others have empty rooms in our homes. And, of course, there are all sorts of things being done that bring great dishonor and embarrassment to the family name. It is precisely this sense of rebirth that has led us to go to conflict zones like Iraq as Christian peacemakers, just to be with our family.

Steven has grown up in the inner city. In fifteen years, he has seen some hard things and become well-acquainted with violence. But he has been one of my (Shane's) teachers for some time. When he was eight, Steven told me he had been trying to figure out who invented the gun. One day he ran up and said,

"Hey, hey, I figured it out. I know who invented the gun."

"Who?" I asked.

"Satan. Because Satan wants us to destroy each other, and God wants us to love each other."

So when I asked ten-year-old Steven, two days after September 11, what we should do, he grew pensive, and then said, "Well, those people did something very evil."

I nodded. Then Steven went on, "But I always say, 'Two wrongs don't make a right.' It doesn't make sense for us to hurt them back. Besides we are all one big family."

His face brightened and, wide-eyed, he said, "Shane, that means you and me are brothers!"

When the United States invaded Iraq in 2003, we went as Christian peacemakers to be with brothers and sisters who were suffering. We felt the love and hospitality of family in Iraq. On the treacherous journey out of Baghdad, one of our cars had a very bad accident. The first Iraqi civilians who came along the road stopped and, risking their lives as jets flew overhead, drove us into a little town called Rutba. There we were met by townspeople and doctors who explained that their hospital had been bombed. With tears in their eyes, they set up a makeshift clinic and literally saved the lives of our friends.

The doctor said to us, "Here it doesn't matter if you are Iraqi or American, Christian or Muslim; we take care of you as our sisters and brothers." Later when we tried to give him money, he refused, insisting that they only took care of us as friends. If we continued to work for peace and to tell the story of what happened in Rutba, the doctor said, that was enough.

The incredible hospitality of that village became a sign of God's love to me (Jonathan). The more I told that story, I realized it was a modern-day good Samaritan story. People who had every reason to be our enemies had stopped by the roadside, pulled our friends out of the ditch and saved their lives. My wife, Leah, and I came back to the United States and started Rutba House, a new monastic community where we try to practice every day the borderless familial love that we experienced in Rutba.

The cry of the Lord's Prayer reminds us of our vocation as children of God, orphans adopted into the family of Yahweh. While the lineage of Jesus is riddled with memories of adultery, imperfection, lying, scheming and murder, the climax is the coming of Emmanuel (God with us). God comes and dwells among us as a Big Brother whom we can emulate. From him we learn to pray, "Our Father in heaven."

Hallowed Be Your Name, Your Kingdom Come . . .

"The kingdom of God is at hand," Jesus says when he appears on the scene in Galilee. Jesus claims that the whole history of Israel is somehow made complete in him. It's a pretty crazy thing to say—unless you're God. Jesus is talking about Israel, the people God called from among all the nations of the world to bear the name of the one true God. And Jesus says the story of this people and their God is somehow summed up in his life. The coming kingdom means that God's name will be made holy among the nations.

I (Jonathan) have a friend, rooted in the black church, who tells me that when white folks talk about "shaping Christian community," what they're really trying to do is find a way to admit that faith is political. The prayer that Jesus taught us to pray won't let us get away with saying otherwise. From its very beginning we're asking for a kingdom—a political reality—right here on earth.

The word *gospel* that Jesus uses to name his message is a political term, used before the writing of the New Testament to refer to the good news that an emperor had won a battle and extended his reign into new lands. Whatever spiritual readings of "kingdom" we might imagine, it's hard to get around the fact that kingdoms are political. And politics is about how a community lives together.

In the Walltown neighborhood of Durham, North Carolina, where I (Jonathan) live, there's a fellow named Andre who hangs out on the street. Andre struggles with mental illness. And he drinks too much. Sometimes he goes missing for weeks at a time. After one such absence, I saw Andre and hollered a greeting to him. "How you been?" I asked.

"You want to talk about theology don't you?" Andre replied.

"Well, sure, I'm always glad to talk theology. What's on your mind?"

Sometimes Andre raps when he talks. With hands flying up and down, he'll set a beat for his poetic speech. This particular day, Andre captured a crucial insight in four short lines. "I'm a Muslim because/Islam is about how you live/Christianity is about what's in your heart/But Islam is about how you live."

There's a story Malcolm X tells in his autobiography about how he received a letter from his brother while he was in prison. "If you want to get out of prison," the letter said, "stop smoking and don't eat pork." Though he didn't yet know that his brother was introducing him to the Nation of Islam, Malcolm X was captivated by the idea that there might be practices that would free him from a life of incarceration. More than religion, Malcolm knew that he needed a new way of life.

I thought about Malcolm when Andre told me why he was a Muslim, and I told him that I believe real Christianity offers the same thing—a whole new way of life. To pray "hallowed be your name" is to ask that the God who comes near to us would make us into a community that could be called holy. It is, in short, to believe that we have been made part of the people called Israel.

Sometimes we Christians have to work to remember this. Of all the peoples of the world, God chose Israel to be God's own. God revealed the law to Israel, patiently insisting that it was to be a road for them to walk in, a way that leads to life. The life the law outlined for Israel was to be a light to the nations. The beauty of Israel's life together was meant as a witness to the way our Creator made all people to live. To know the life of Israel was to know the love of Israel's God.

This intimate relationship with a stiff-necked people proved difficult for God. Moses points out what a mess God got into in Exodus 32:31. After the people have turned from God, rejected God's way and built a golden calf to worship, God is ready to simply get rid of them and start over. But Moses reminds God that God has already branded this people. God's name is on them. Their destruction will mean the ridicule of God's name among the nations. The predicament is clear: unless these people are made holy, God's name cannot be made holy. God's name and the life of this community are married so closely together that they simply cannot be separated.

So it is that Israel's God, maker of heaven and earth, takes on human flesh—Jewish flesh, that is. Jesus, God-in-Jewish-flesh, said that he came not to abolish the law but to fulfill it (Matthew 5:17). Jesus came to do what Israel could not do on their own—to live a life worthy of God's name. In doing so, Jesus defeated the power of Satan, the enemy of all true community. Resisting the devil, Jesus lived the way of God's law. Indeed, Jesus called himself the Way. To live this Way is to become part of Jesus' body—that body politic in which Israel's way of life is graciously opened to all the peoples of the earth. "Hallowed be your name," then, is a prayer that God would teach us to live a new way of life.

But we cannot be too quick to claim Jesus' politics as our own (whether we're Republicans or Democrats or militant jihadists). "*Your* kingdom come" is always a reminder that we do not possess the kingdom as our own. We have been invited to become living members of Christ's body. But the body still belongs to Christ.

Learning the way of Jesus is not as simple as asking "What would Jesus do?" knowing that Jesus would do the good and decent thing (and assuming that we are the sort of people

ANIMA CHRISTI

Soul of Christ, sanctify me
Body of Christ, save me
Blood of Christ, inebriate me
Water from the side of Christ,
  wash me
Passion of Christ, strengthen me
O good Jesus, hear me
Within Thy wounds hide me
Suffer me not to be separated
  from Thee
From the malicious enemy defend me
In the hour of my death call me
And bidst me come to Thee
That with Thy saints I may
  praise Thee
Forever and ever. Amen.

30

who already know what is good and decent). As members of Christ's body, we must first learn to ask "What *did* Jesus do?" This much is clear: Jesus announced a kingdom not of this world—a kingdom whose politics run so counter to politics as usual that the "powers that be" decided they'd rather have Jesus dead. Just as important is what Jesus did not do. He didn't resist, but "humbled himself / by becoming obedient to death—even death on a cross" (Philippians 2:8). The way of Jesus is not a proposal for how to take over the nation-state and make it Christian. It is, rather, a lesson in learning not to take over—to be a community where we find a new way of life by giving ourselves for others.

We have a friend who is a Medical Missions Sister and lives in a recovery community in North Philadelphia. Together with fifty or so recovering drug addicts, she tends an award-winning garden, cooks meals, keeps house, studies Scripture, offers hospitality to neighbors, and works for justice and peace in the city. She often talks about how she has learned from her community that conversion is about developing new habits for living.

Drug addicts know that getting saved is not just about having your past sins forgiven. It's also about receiving the gift of a life free from the power of addiction. Even though our friend has never used drugs, she says her community helps her see how she is an addict—enslaved by selfishness and pride. She is discovering a new way of life in this community of recovery and conversion. Along with her brothers and sisters there, she calls the community New Jerusalem Now.

In the book of Revelation the New Jerusalem descends from heaven to become a city on earth. It is the fulfillment of our common prayer: "your kingdom come . . . on earth as it is in heaven." The kingdom is not some place that our souls are taken away to when we die. It is, instead, an order that comes to earth—right here among us who call ourselves daughters and sons of God.

Praying back to God the prayer that Jesus taught us to pray, we get used to saying God's words as our words. We form habits of hoping that our lives will look more like God's life. And at the same time, we give ourselves over to an extended family of all God's children, in which we learn to give ourselves as Christ gave himself for us.

As we've talked with God this way, we've also begun to see that we gain a community of others who are learning to give themselves for us. Which is another way of saying that we find our lives in Christ. We become the kind of community that is the answer to our request: Make your name holy, Father, by bringing your kingdom here on earth. Christian community is the gift of a life that is worthy of God's name. Forgetting ourselves, we become the sort of joyful people who hallow God's name by how we live with one another.

I (Jonathan) talked with a recent college graduate who told me that she was confused. She felt as if her very good education left her with two options: either work hard and get rich or work hard and save the world. As a Christian she knew that greed wasn't a very good motivation to live by. But she also felt uncomfortable about setting out to save the world. Hadn't Jesus already done that?

We've felt this same confusion. Given the options, it's often hard to know what to do. But the most important thing about the prayer Jesus teaches may be that it invites us into new options. We don't have to give into greed or work as if everything depends on us. When the options are "get rich" or "save the world," we can respond with, "I want to become part of the people who ask for God's kingdom to come in their life together." We can find our identity not in our work or our causes, but in "Our Father in heaven."

2

Begging for God's Economy

JESUS DOESN'T DILLY-DALLY NEARLY as long as we have, talking about context and explaining his terms. When teaching his disciples to pray, Jesus moves straight from asking for the kingdom to begging for God's economy. "Give us today our daily bread," he prays, "and forgive us our debts, as we also have forgiven our debtors." Jesus knows that if we're asking God for a way of life, we have to deal with money.

Some years ago we heard that the city of New York had begun passing antihomeless legislation that criminalized people who did not have homes. Police were arresting people for sleeping in public. These laws were not accompanied by housing and other provisions for people who slept on the streets. They simply made it illegal to be homeless. It wasn't the first time we had heard this story. Some years before, similar ordinances had gone on the books in Philadelphia. Along with friends from the streets and from our community, I (Shane) had been involved with contesting those ordinances in Philly. And we had won. When we heard about what was happening in New York, we knew this unjust law could be beat.

So I went up to New York and got arrested for sleeping on the sidewalk. With help from some pro bono lawyers, we took the case to court and won. The court called the law into question and ordered the city to pay punitive damages. So, a few months later, I got a check for $10,000 from the City of New York. Now, the money didn't belong to me. It didn't really belong to any of us in Philadelphia. It belonged to the homeless of New York. So we had to find a way to get it to them.

At that time we had been studying the biblical concept of Jubilee and praying for a better understanding of what God's economy looks like. A campaign to forgive African nations their debts (Jubilee 2000) had awakened many of us to this ancient idea in Hebrew Scripture. The rock star Bono was meeting together with conservative senator Jesse Helms to read the book of Leviticus. We knew something interesting was going on. So we turned to the Scriptures ourselves and read the sabbath legislation.

On the seventh day Israel was to rest, just as God had rested on the seventh day of creation. And on the seventh year they were to give their land a rest, trusting God to sustain them. And after seven years times seven—on the fiftieth year—they were to declare a Jubilee. Debts would be forgiven. Land that had been sold would be returned to its original owner. Prisoners would be set free. Once in every generation, the playing field would be leveled as a guard against injustice in the beloved community of God's people.

That's what Leviticus said. But we found little evidence that God's people had ever really practiced Jubilee. It seemed so far from everything we knew about fiscal responsibility and good stewardship. But it was also compelling. So compelling, in fact, that we started asking this question: What might a Jubilee celebration on Wall Street look like?

One of the folks in the study on sabbath economics announced that he had $10,000 that had formerly been invested in stocks which he wanted to redistribute among God's people. So we sent out Jubilee invitations to Christian communities and to the homeless in New York. In each case, the invitations had cash from the growing Jubilee Fund stapled to them, along with a call to join us on Wall Street where the rest of the money would be redistributed.

It happened on a Monday morning. Some of us were dressed like professionals going to their offices. Some of us looked homeless, and some of us were homeless. Some of us were dressed like clowns (this was a celebration after all). At the appointed time I climbed up on the statue of George Washington and announced through a bull horn that some of us had been set free from poverty and some of us had been set free from greed, but all of us were here as the family of God to celebrate Jubilee—redistribution of that which had been unjustly hoarded. Our friend Sister Margaret raised a shofar to her mouth and blew the traditional Jewish horn. With that,

Dear God,
Please make all the poor people rich.
And all the rich people poor.
Then bring us all back to medium so we will take better care of each other.
Amen.

ten-year-old boy, Philadelphia

thousands of one-dollar bills and pieces of small change were tossed into the air and poured onto the busy street in front of the Stock Exchange. For thirty minutes or so one Monday morning, business as usual was interrupted on Wall Street by the celebration of God's new economy.

Give Us Today . . .

When we pray "give us today our daily bread. And forgive us our debts, as we also have forgiven our debtors," we've learned that we're asking God for Jubilee. Our prayer comes out of the story of Israel, and so we are never able to forget the essential connection between God's provision of manna in the wilderness and the way of living that God revealed to Israel at Mt. Sinai. This way is not only a new politics. It is also a new economy. It is, before all else, an economy of providence.

In the wilderness God teaches Israel to trust that they will receive their daily bread. Each day they are to gather enough manna for that day. And there is enough for everyone. But when some try to hoard, the extra manna is eaten up by maggots (Exodus 16). The lesson is clear: God's way of life includes an economy of radical redistribution in which "the one who gathered much did not have too much, and the one who gathered little did not have too little" (Exodus 16:18). It is in the context of laying out this way of life that God introduces Israel to the concept of Jubilee. Those who have been trained to trust God for provision are the only people who will ever believe that Jubilee is a good idea. Otherwise, it looks like losing everything you have worked so hard to earn. But if we never earn anything—if everything is gift—then it begins to make sense that God would want to redistribute gifts as a guard against injustice in a broken and sinful world.

At his first recorded sermon in his hometown, Jesus stood up in a synagogue and declared that the Jubilee was fulfilled in him. "The Spirit of the Lord is on me," Jesus read from Isaiah, "because he has anointed me / to proclaim good news to the poor / . . . to proclaim the year of the Lord's favor" (Luke 4:18-19). The year of the Lord's favor *is* the year of Jubilee. And then, the Scripture tells us, Jesus closed the book, sat down and said, "Today this scripture is fulfilled in your hearing."

What does it mean for Jesus to say that the Jubilee is fulfilled in him? How does a new economy get summed up in an individual? We do not have to read any farther than the second and fourth chapters of Acts to see the Holy Spirit, third person of the Trinity, descending on Jesus' followers and literally making them members of Christ's body as they are joined in community. "Those who accepted his message were baptized, and about three thousand were added to their number that day. . . . All the believers were together and had everything in common. They sold property and possessions to give to anyone who had need" (Acts 2:41, 44-45).

For the early church, to be baptized into the body of Christ meant initiation into the economic sharing of a new community. The Scriptures go on to say that "there were no needy persons among them" (Acts 4:34). They ended poverty. One of the signs of Pentecost, the birthday of the church, is that poverty came to an end because God's children learned how to love one another as brothers and sisters.

Our Daily Bread

One of the beautiful and peculiar rituals of the church is this thing we call the Eucharist or the Lord's Supper. Some folks call it a "mystery," and there is certainly much to contemplate in this divine meal. But one of the things we so often forget is that for the early Christians, the Eucharist was not just a sacred tradition but was part of a lively "Love Feast" in which food was shared with the poor. As we break off a small piece of bread and take a modest sip from the cup, we rest assured that there will be enough for everyone.

But even early on, the young church starts to forget the point, and Paul scolds them for desecrating the Table of the Lord (1 Corinthians 11). Pastors often read part of this text from Corinthians and invite people to prepare their hearts for Communion by confessing sins and reconciling with brothers or sisters before coming to the Table, both of which are important. But Paul's point is even more fundamental. Some people in Corinth were coming to the Communion table hungry while others were stuffed full of food and drink. How dare they claim to be family! Listen to Paul's words:

> Your meetings do more harm than good. In the first place, I hear that when you come together as a church, there are divisions among you. . . . When you come together, it is not the Lord's Supper you eat, for when you are eating, some of you go ahead with your own private suppers. As a result, one person remains hungry and another gets drunk. . . . Do you despise the church of God by humiliating those who have nothing? What shall I say to you? Shall I praise you? Certainly not in this matter! (1 Corinthians 11:17-18, 20-22)

Throughout the history of the church, Christians have recognized that we cannot pray "Our father" together on Sunday and deny bread to our brothers and sisters on Monday. But we live in difficult days. The hungry are not just hungry. Often they are also our enemies. Drug addiction and mental illness make many who are hungry hard to deal with. They threaten us. Others have been hungry for so long that they are angry, even at those of us who want to help. We worry about how to protect ourselves from them while at the same time feeling guilty for our complicity in their poverty. So we give to charities. And charities become the brokers for our compassion toward the poor.

The problem with this is that we never get to know the poor. Though we have been made children of God together with them in Jesus Christ, we never sit down to eat with our hungry brothers and sisters. We never hear their stories. We never learn to see

> *"Father, forgive me the bread I've stolen from my brother."*
>
> **St. Vincent de Paul**

the world through their eyes. Many Christians are concerned about the breakdown of nuclear families (and rightly so), but we often just accept the breakdown of God's family. We live like teenagers in a high school cafeteria—some of us eating at one table (*our* table), while others eat at another table (quite often, the soup kitchen's table). What we miss is the gift of God's new economy. And with it, our brothers and sisters on "the other side."

While we have learned a lot from teachers in the church and a number of fine academic institutions, we both met some of our best teachers in Love Park. When we were students at Eastern College (now Eastern University), there was a group who went downtown every Saturday to share meals with homeless folks in the park. We told people that we were spending our weekends with friends at the YACHT club—YACHT stood for Youth Against Complacency and Homelessness Today. (You might say it was a different kind of yacht club.) Over sandwiches that we made at Eastern's cafeteria, we'd talk with our friends on the street about those things you're not supposed to talk about at dinner—God and politics. Many of them had whole chapters of Scripture memorized. And their faith ran deeper than our limited experience could fathom.

These were brothers and sisters who struggled to survive on the streets of Philly. Our relationships in the YACHT club taught us what the early church expressed in one of its main symbols, a boat. Like sailors at sea (or yachters in a bay, I guess), we're all in this together. If you don't like someone on the boat, well, the alternative is a deep, blue sea. We learn to survive together or we sink to the bottom alone. That's the economics of the church in a nutshell.

Since our little celebration of Jubilee on Wall Street, we've continued to ask what God's economy can look like in everyday practice. (Clowning on Wall Street is fun, but you can't do it every day.) Friends across the globe, rich and poor, have begun to dream what it would look like to reimagine our offerings as God intended them to be—instruments of a redistributive economy. We considered how the early church brought their offerings and laid them at the feet of the apostles to be redistributed to folks as they had need. And we came up with something beautiful and small—the Relational Tithe (RT).[1]

The RT is a network of reborn friends around the world, organized in little cells like a body, taking care of each other. Like the early church, we bring our offerings and needs before the community and share them. Unlike the early church, we have a blog and can wire money across the globe. We pool 10 percent of our income into a common fund. Regularly, needs of our neighborhoods and villages are brought before the community, and we meet them as we are able. Meanwhile, we are building relationships which tear through the economic walls that formerly divided us, all the time trusting that we can do more together than we could alone. Together, we've helped friends get cars, keep their utilities on, create new jobs, send kids to summer camps, throw birthday parties and send people on their first vacation. And it all happens through relationships. No one is giving or receiving who is not grounded in sincere friendships.

When the tsunami hit Southeast Asia in 2004, two folks from RT went to Thailand. They brought the needs of people they met before the community, and we were able to help repair fences, boats and playgrounds (and even got a write-up in the *Bangkok Post,* one of Thailand's most prominent newspapers).

Make us worthy, Lord, to serve our fellow men throughout the world, who live and die in poverty and hunger. Give them today, through our hands, their daily bread and through our understanding love, give peace and joy. Amen.

Missionaries of Charity

After the 2005 hurricane hit the Gulf of Mexico, folks from RT and other friends sent supplies and people to Louisiana, on a bus running off veggie oil (which was particularly delightful at a time when gas prices were sky-high). RT also organized a network of families and communities who opened up their homes to folks displaced by the hurricane. We've been inspired by God's vision for a human family with a divine Parent who has a big wallet and a lot of love.

Relational Tithe is a group of about fifty people scattered around the world who've begun to explore God's economy. We know a little church in Oregon that has about forty members. They don't own a building or pay any full-time staff. But they are serious about tithing. And they use that money to bless people who are in need. In any given year, this little church gives tens of thousands of dollars away to people they know and love.

The kingdom that we beg God to send "on earth as it is in heaven" is a kingdom of generosity. And it is contagious. When Jesus proclaimed it to one woman, she brought expensive perfume and poured it on his feet. Some of the disciples were outraged. Why hadn't she sold the fragrance and given the money to the poor? "The poor," Jesus answered, "you will always have with you." He was quoting Deuteronomy: "There will always be poor people in the land. Therefore I command you to be openhanded toward those of your people who are poor and needy in your land" (Deuteronomy 15:11).

To live God's way of life in the world is to know that the poor are our brothers and sisters. If they are poor, then we are poor. But we are also rich because our Father owns the cattle on a thousand hillsides. And our God is able to rain bread from heaven. Our task is to take enough for the day, be thankful for it and pass the rest along to whoever may have need. What if there were a little group like the RT or our friends in Oregon in every city and town?

After the party was over at Wall Street and the police had asked us to leave, I (Jonathan) got on the subway with James. James is a recovering addict who used to be homeless. I asked what the experience had been like for him. "I pulled a huge stack of dollar bills out of my pocket, and I thought, 'Man, that's a lot of money!' " James said, laughing. "I threw it up in the air and watched it float back to the ground. Then I bent over and picked up a couple for myself, because we all need a little something." That's the good news of God's economy: we all need a little something, and God offers it to us in the new economy that we pray for.

3

Temptations Along the Way

AS THE ISRAELITES WERE BEING LED OUT OF EGYPT, they began to grumble of hunger, saying, "If only we had stayed back in Egypt where we sat around pots of meat and ate all the food we wanted." Temptation is part of the exodus adventure. Temptation is a sign that we are still on our way to the Promised Land. It reminds us that we have left something good for something better. So Jesus teaches us to pray, "Lead us not into temptation, but deliver us from the evil one."

Lead Us Not into Temptation

The moment we are no longer tempted by the "pots of meat" the empire offers, we should be concerned—for if we can't feel the temptation, we have probably given in to it. Christians are not people who are no longer tempted but people who have seen enough of God to be able to resist the kingdom of this world. Our eyes have caught a glimpse of the Promised Land, and it is so dazzling that we can no longer settle for what the empire has to offer.

Isn't it interesting that one of the first things Jesus does after his baptism is head into the desert to be tempted? It's striking that the temptations he faces are not just personal sins like sleeping around or drinking too much. The most attractive temptations are not just the bad things but the subtle distortions of good things, like miracles. One of my (Shane) mentors once told me: "Beware of the almost good, for if the devil can't get you to do bad things, he will get you to settle for the almost good, just short of the good that God has for you." And if the tempter can't steal our soul, perhaps he will just keep us busy with "important" work that pulls us away from community, reconciliation and living.

We hesitate to use an illustration from the CBS miniseries on Jesus, but the temptation scenes were fantastic (if you haven't seen it, we recommend reading the book). The tempter comes to Jesus in many forms—a businessman in a three-piece suit with an attractive business deal, a dazzling woman ready to swoon at some miraculous sign and, finally, a starving little girl who begs Jesus to turn stones into bread so she can eat. His response is unbelievable. Jesus knows he can end the groaning bellies of the world's starving children, but he resists and says that he will trust in the church.

That must have been hard—and probably still is. The last visit from the tempter comes in the Garden of Gethsemane, just before Jesus is crucified. The devil tells him, "They do not understand your cross, Jesus. They will never understand your cross." And he shows Jesus glimpses of the Crusades

and holy wars—of all of the blood shed in the name of God—
and asks Jesus if he still wants to die for that. Then Jesus is
taken by the soldiers. Perhaps that was the last temptation.

Do you ever wonder how we heard of the temptations Jesus faced in his solitary moments? He must have practiced
the discipline of humble confession even after the resurrection, knowing it would be good for his goofball disciples to
see his vulnerabilities.

"Lead us not into temptation . . ." These are the words of
humble little people who know they are neither beyond the
grasps of temptation nor beyond the
clutches of evil. One thing we have
learned from conservative Christian believers and from progressive
social activists is that community
can be built around a common self-

"I no longer fear God, but I love him."

St. Anthony of the Desert

righteousness or around a common brokenness. Both are
magnetic and contagious. People are drawn toward folks who
have it all together (or have figured out how to look like they
do). People are also drawn toward folks who know they don't
have it all together and are not willing to fake it. Christianity can be built around isolating ourselves from evildoers and
sinners, creating a community of religious super-piety. Christianity can also be built around joining with the broken sinners
and evildoers of our world crying out to God, groaning for
grace. That's the Christianity we have fallen in love with.

In Luke 18, Jesus tells the remarkable story of the Pharisee
and tax collector praying. The Pharisee stands up and thanks
God he is not like the evildoers. The tax collector cannot even
lift his head, but beats his chest and cries out, "God, have

mercy on me, a sinner." It's the tax collector, not the Pharisee, who goes home justified that day.

That stuff Jesus warned us to be aware of, the "yeast of the Pharisees," is so infectious today among liberals and conservatives. Conservatives stand up and thank God that they are not like the homosexuals, the Muslims, the liberals. Liberals stand up and thank God that they are not like the warmongers, the yuppies, the conservatives. It is a similar self-righteousness, just different definitions of "evil-doing." Both can paralyze us in judgment and guilt, and rob us of life. Rather than separating ourselves from everyone we consider impure, Jesus seems to say that we are better off beating our chests and praying that God would be merciful enough to save us from this present ugliness and make our lives so beautiful that people cannot resist the mercy.

Some Christians say, "If people knew all my struggles and weaknesses, they would never want to be a Christian." But it may be that the opposite is true. If people really knew what idiots we are, in all our brokenness and vulnerability, they would know that they could give this thing a shot too. Christianity is for sick people. The evangelical troubadour Rich Mullins used to say, "Whenever people say, 'Christians are hypocrites,' I say, 'Duh, every time we come together as a community we are confessing that we are hypocrites, weaklings in need of God and each other.' " We know that we cannot do life alone, and the good news is that we don't have to.

We usually finish the prayer that Jesus taught us by saying, "For yours is the kingdom and the power and the glory forever. Amen." These are important words for those of us who begin to dream the dreams of God. We need to hear

ROMERO'S PRAYER

It helps, now and then, to step back and take a long view.
The kingdom is not only beyond our efforts,
it is even beyond our vision.
We accomplish in our lifetime only a tiny fraction
of the magnificent enterprise that is God's work.
Nothing we do is complete, which is a way of saying
that the kingdom always lies beyond us.
No statement says all that could be said.
No prayer fully expresses our faith.
No confession brings perfection.
No pastoral visit brings wholeness.
No program accomplishes the church's mission.
No set of goals and objectives includes everything.
This is what we are about.
We plant the seeds that one day will grow.
We water seeds already planted,
knowing that they hold future promise.
We lay foundations that will need further development.
We provide yeast that produces far beyond our capabilities.
We cannot do everything, and there is a sense of liberation
in realizing that. This enables us to do something,
and to do it very well. It may be incomplete,
but it is a beginning, a step along the way,
an opportunity for the Lord's grace to enter and do the rest.
We may never see the end results, but that is the difference
between the master builder and the worker.
We are workers, not master builders; ministers, not messiahs.
We are prophets of a future not our own.
Amen.

Archbishop Oscar Romero

them because we can quickly find ourselves thinking we have moved beyond the filthy rotten system and into the promised land of our own righteousness. We can begin to trust in our own holiness (which means we are "set apart") and think that in our own strength we can conspire a countercultural movement. We forget that the end of our prayer is a confession that the kingdom and power and glory are God's. Sometimes we just want a little secret stash of the glory. Sometimes we can stand up and beat our chests like the tax collector just so other people see how humble we are. And that is dangerous.

Unfortunately, many Christians seem to be hoping that the kingdom of God will come in triumphal greatness, expanding God's territory and taking over the world with glory and power. But that's the very temptation that Jesus faced in the desert—the temptation to do spectacular things like fling himself from the temple or turn stones into bread, to shock the masses with his miracles or dazzle them with his power. And yet he resists. The church has always faced the same temptation, from Constantine's sword to now.

But amid all the assumptions about growth and development that saturate our culture, we want to suggest something a little different: God's kingdom grows smaller and smaller as it takes over the world. Mother Teresa offers us the brilliant glimpse of hope that lies in little things: "We can do no great things, only small things with great love. It is not how much you do but how much love you put into doing it." Above the front door inside The Simple Way, there is a sign that says: "Today . . . Small things with great love (or don't open the door)."

It is very easy to fall in love with the great things, whether we are revolutionaries or church strategists. But we must never simply fall in love with our vision or five-year plan. We must never fall in love with "the revolution" or "the movement." We can easily become so genuinely driven by our vision for church growth, community or social justice that we forget the little things, like caring for those around us.

There is a brilliant truth we have come to see, largely inspired by theologian and fellow resister Dietrich Bonhoeffer. In his book *Life Together,* Bonhoeffer observes that the person who loves their dream of community will destroy community, but the person who loves those around them will create community. Many congregations are in love with their mission and vision, and rip one another apart in committee meetings trying to attain it. And many social activists tear each other up and burn themselves out fighting for a better world while forgetting that the seeds of that world are right next to them.

We have a God who enters the world through smallness— as a baby refugee. We have a God who values the little offering of a single coin from a widow over the megacharity of millionaires. We have a God who speaks through little people—a stuttering spokesman named Moses; the stubborn donkey of Balaam; a lying brothel owner named Rahab; an adulterous king named David; a ragtag bunch of disciples who betrayed, doubted and denied; and a converted terrorist named Paul.

Alluding to the Old Testament story where God speaks through a donkey, Rich Mullins used to say, "God spoke to Balaam through his ass, and God's been speaking through asses ever since."[1] So if God should choose to use us, we shouldn't think too highly of ourselves. And we should never assume that God cannot use someone, no matter how ornery or awkward they appear to be. Because, after all, God spoke to Balaam through his ass.

One of the communities we have bumped into is a bunch of middle-aged parents and their kids living in the suburbs who had decided to do a little experiment in community. They started sharing garden tools and lawn mowers, doing laundry together and sharing machines. They found it was more fun to do their laundry together and spend time together while they waited (which poor folks have known for a long time).

Before long, they had a community garden and had set up a way to do cooperative childcare. A few of them even moved in together. It felt so natural. Eventually, they made the front page of the newspaper, and one of the folks who had started it said, "Isn't that weird? What we are doing is front-page news. It just seemed to make sense." If God's kingdom looks radical, it is only an indictment on the sort of Christianity we have settled for. Sharing our food with the hungry, opening our homes to the homeless, reconciling with our enemies— these are what Christianity has always been.

Deliver Us from the Evil One

It's interesting that Jesus does not teach us to pray, "End evil," or "Rid the world of evildoers," but "deliver us from the evil one." We are not taught to pray that we be kept from pain. Suffering is the inevitable plight of Christians who are disturbed by the discomfort of their neighbors. And Jesus knew all too well that the way of the cross is not the way of safety and comfort. For Jesus and nearly all his disciples, it meant horrific suffering and martyrdom. Jesus did not rid the world of evil, nor was he delivered from evil. Instead, Jesus was handed over to evil that he might deliver us. Evil seemed to triumph at the cross, but evil did not have the final word. God raised Jesus from the dead.

Most of us live in such fear of death that it's no small wonder few people believe in resurrection anymore. Sometimes people ask us if we are scared, living in the inner city. We usually reply with something like, "We're more afraid of shopping malls." The Scriptures say that we should not fear those things that can destroy the body, but we are to fear that which can destroy the soul (Matthew 10:28). While the ghettos may have their share of violence and crime, the posh suburbs are home to more subtle demonic forces—numbness, complacency and comfort. These are the powers that can eat away at our souls.

Our mothers have some things to say about safety. As they have watched us move into the inner city and travel to Iraq with God's hand evidently in the midst of it all, they tell us they have learned a lot about faith, safety and risk. It has not been easy, but Shane's mom recently said, "I have come to see that we Christians are not called to safety, but we are promised that God will be with us when we are in danger. And there is no better place to be than in the hand of God." Perhaps the most dangerous place for a Christian to be is in safety and comfort.

So whether it gets us awards or gets us killed, we have chosen to follow Jesus and to cry out with his prayer. His last words on the cross were a cry to his Father, "Into your hands I commit my spirit." We want to live and die with the same resolve. We will dance the revolution of God till they kill us, then we will dance some more.

When we say "Amen" at the closing of the Lord's Prayer, we are proclaiming, "So be it." Dorothy Day, pioneer of The Catholic Worker Movement that has birthed hospitality houses and intentional communities around the world, looked at the world and looked at the Scriptures and could not help but ask, "Have we even begun to be Christians?" Saying "Amen," we commit ourselves to be the instruments that enact God's kingdom on earth. It is not the end, but the beginning. Let us begin to be Christians again. Amen.

Part Two

JOHN 17

Father, the hour has come. Glorify your Son, that your Son may glorify you. . . .

I have revealed you to those whom you gave me out of the world. They were yours; you gave them to me and they have obeyed your word. Now they know that everything you have given me comes from you. For I gave them the words you gave me and they accepted them. They knew with certainty that I came from you, and they believed that you sent me. I pray for them. I am not praying for the world, but for those you have given me, for they are yours. . . .

My prayer is not that you take them out of the world but that you protect them from the evil one. They are not of the world, even as I am not of it. Sanctify them by the truth; your word is truth. As you sent me into the world, I have sent them into the world. (John 17:1, 6-9, 15-18)

4

Love and Unity for the Sake of the World

SOMEWHERE IN A BOOK ON PRAYER, we want to say that where we pray makes a difference. This is probably as good a place as any to say it. While we are still working on "praying without ceasing," we have in our communities little corners and chapels where folks can also pull aside to pray. Plastered on the walls in some of these spaces are the names of people and events—the deep groanings of our hearts over the years. It's sort of a visual history of memories—some beautiful, some tragic.

One of my (Shane's) favorite places to pray was in the chapel of our old house that burned down in 2007. We had fixed up this old "abandominium" drug-house (which we bought for $1 from the city), and the house next to it was still abandoned.

So we created a secret passageway into the still-vacant row house next door, fully rigged with a bookshelf that opened up a passageway into Narnia (okay, not Narnia, but it was almost as magical).

That's where I would pray each night. Sometimes I felt a little subversive sneaking into an abandoned house we didn't own to be with God. It was a bit romantic. And it was a little scary, as a young lady in our neighborhood had been killed in the house a few years earlier. One of the first things we did was sneak through an opening in the house with an Episcopal priest friend and pray over the space, dedicating it to the work of God. Sometimes as I prayed there, I'd notice the traces of the old world, like an empty heroine bag in the corner of the chapel.

One night I read about how Jesus says we are to go into our closet to pray. As I did a little more reading on that verse, I found that the word often translated "closet" actually means secret chamber. It was the inner room of the house, one of the only places that was hidden or locked. And you can imagine what happened in the secret chamber—some of the most beautiful things in the world . . . and some of the ugliest. So it is with the secret chambers of our homes and lives and neighborhoods.

The prayers we're learning to pray have led us deeper into God's reality in the particular communities where we live. In the Kensington neighborhood of Philadelphia and the Walltown neighborhood of Durham, the Lord's Prayer calls us out of the empire's death-dealing systems and into a whole new kingdom.

We pray in the shadows of the empire. Because we see

firsthand the pain of politics as usual, we hear good news in the promise of a new kingdom with attentive ears. Because we can see economic divisions written on the faces of our neighbors and our sisters and brothers in community, we rejoice in the gift of daily bread. We pray the Lord's Prayer and hear a call to become a new society because of where we are. Our neighborhoods cry out for the kingdom to come.

It's worth noting: we're not the only Christians in America who look at the signs of the times today and see the need for social engagement. I (Jonathan) saw five different preachers

---

RADIATING CHRIST

Dear Jesus, help us to spread your fragrance everywhere we go.

Flood our souls with your spirit and life.

Penetrate and possess our whole being so utterly that our lives may only be a radiance of yours.

Shine through us, and be so in us, that every soul we come in contact with may feel your presence in our soul.

Let them look up and see no longer us but only Jesus!

Stay with us, and then we shall begin to shine as you shine; so to shine as to be a light to others; the light O Jesus, will be all from you, none of it will be ours; it will be you, shining on others through us.

Let us thus praise you in the way you love best by shining on those around us.

Let us preach you without preaching, not by words but by our example, by the catching force, the sympathetic influence of what we do.

The evident fullness of the love our hearts bear to you.

Amen.

---

interviewed on CNN over an Easter weekend. Now, maybe this happens all the time on CNN, but I was kind of surprised to see five preachers on a news show. And I was even more struck to hear that they were talking about politics. On Easter weekend CNN wanted to ask some prominent pastors about the politics of Jesus. I don't know whether it's still considered impolite to talk about religion and politics at dinner, but cable news seems to think it's perfectly all right to do so before dinner. Maybe things aren't what they used to be.

But even as more and more people acknowledge that Jesus isn't apolitical, there doesn't seem to be a popular consensus on what God's politics look like. Together with the whole church we pray for God's kingdom to come on earth as it is in heaven. But we still have to ask, *How* does God's kingdom come? One of the greatest dangers for the church, especially amid a buzz that our faith has to be "relevant" to the culture, is losing the peculiarity of our politics. The great challenge is maintaining the distinctiveness of God's kingdom, which is so radically nonconforming to the patterns of this world.

So it makes sense that Jesus does not pray for the world but for the people whom God has called to be set apart from the world. We talk a lot about how the church's mission is to create a new culture—a culture where it is easier for people to be good. But just because our gospel gets political doesn't mean it happens on the empire's terms.

The question is not whether we are prolife, but how consistently do we honor life? One of the most important questions for the church today is not whether Christianity is political but how Christianity is political. How does Jubilee economics take over Wall Street? How does the peace of Christ bring an end to wars and rumors of wars? Yes, Jesus came preaching a kingdom. And God cares about everything they talk about in Washington. But the Bible doesn't seem to talk like they talk in D.C. Jesus never prays for his party to come into power. He doesn't even try to win the ear of policymakers. Instead, Jesus prays that the church would be one as the Trinity is one. The politics of Jesus are very peculiar and upside-down—or rightside-up.

Jesus humbled himself and did *not* take charge of things by force. He is moving world history as a lamb, not a conqueror. To be a Christian is to follow suit. This is where a conversation from the movie *Romero,* about Oscar Romero, the late archbishop of San Salvador, speaks clearly:

> *Romero:* You don't pray anymore.
> *Revolutionary priest:* I still pray, all of the time.
> *Romero:* Then why do you carry a gun?

When we buy into the politics of this world, we cannot see how prayer makes a difference in us or in our enemies. Maybe a gun *is* all that can save us. But becoming the answer to Jesus' prayer is about learning a new kind of politics.

Many preachers have noted that Jesus announces a political platform in his inaugural sermon at Nazareth. The night those five preachers were on CNN, every one of them quoted this passage:

> The Spirit of the Lord is on me,
>   because he has anointed me
>   to proclaim good news to the poor.

He has sent me to proclaim freedom for the prisoners
   and recovery of sight for the blind,
to set the oppressed free,
   to proclaim the year of the Lord's favor. (Luke 4:18-19)

With an announcement like that, it's no wonder that Jesus was able to rally some pretty large crowds among the peasant farmers and even recruit a few revolutionaries to join his band of followers. But folks in the Gospels who thought they understood Jesus' politics were often disappointed. Here was a King who ruled with a towel rather than an iron fist, a King who rode a donkey instead of a warhorse, a King who carried a cross rather than a sword.

Even Jesus' disciples had lots of questions about why Jesus decided to go about things the way he did. Which may be why his farewell address is a lot longer than his inaugural sermon. John 13—17 is Jesus' longest teaching on record. He starts it by washing his disciples' feet and ends it by praying for them—and for us. John 17 is a prayer that helps us see how God means to introduce a new kingdom into the world. Praying it with Jesus in community has taught us a good deal about how we become the answer to our prayers. It's a good prayer to pay attention to since it's Jesus' longest and perhaps one of his last. Here we can hear the deepest groanings of Jesus' heart—for us to experience eternal life before death, for us to be set apart from the patterns of the world, for us to be one as God is one.

Glorify Your Son, That Your Son May Glorify You
Jesus begins his prayer in John 17 by saying that the hour has come. Time is important in John's Gospel. When Jesus'

mother comes to him at Cana to see if he can do something to salvage a wedding party, he says to her: "My hour has not yet come." He doesn't say why the timing is bad. But Jesus is clearly thinking about time. He is on a mission, and it's important to get the timing right. John tells us at the beginning of chapter 13 that "Jesus knew that the hour had come" (v. 1). Jesus begins his prayer in chapter 17 by saying as much to his Father.

But back in John 13, at the beginning of Jesus' farewell address, John tells us what Jesus has been waiting for. "Having loved his own who were in the world, he now showed them the full extent of his love" (John 13:1 NIV). What Jesus calls his "hour" is, evidently, the moment when he has the opportunity to show the whole world the full extent of God's love. Whatever else Jesus might have come to do, this is the main event in John's Gospel. Jesus came to reveal the glory of God's love. So he begins his prayer in chapter 17, "Father, the hour has come. Glorify your Son, that your Son may glorify you."

I (Jonathan) remember hearing John's Gospel read in church when I was a kid. It always seemed a little strange to me that Jesus asked his Father to glorify him. After all, I was a (sometimes) sassy kid, and my momma was always telling me that Jesus was humble and that God wanted me to be humble too. I wanted to be a good kid, so I tried to be humble like Jesus. But what sort of humility teaches you to beg God to glorify you? I had a pretty hard time understanding the glory of God.

Evidently, I'm not the only one. Israel was fascinated by the glory of God, but from all I've read no one really seemed to understand it. Ezekiel said he saw the glory of the Lord, down by the Kebar River in Babylon. He tries for a whole chapter to describe it in an overwhelming barrage of images (Ezekiel 1). But for the life of me, I can't sketch a picture from his description. Isaiah said that the glory of the Lord filled the temple in Jerusalem one day when he was there, and he came out with fire on his tongue. But the glory was still a mystery (Isaiah 6). The tradition, all the way back to Moses, was that no one could see the fullness of God's glory and live. According to Exodus, Moses saw God's backside on Mt. Sinai, and his face glowed so bright that the people couldn't stand to look at him (Exodus 33—34). Israel couldn't imagine seeing the glory of God.

But that's how John *starts* his Gospel—by claiming, "We have seen his glory, the glory of the one and only, who came from the Father, full of grace and truth. . . . No one has ever seen God, but the one and only, who is himself God and is in closest relationship with the Father, has made him known" (John 1:14, 18). From the very beginning of the story, John tells us that, if we watch, we will see God's glory in the life of Jesus. It's an extraordinary claim to make at the beginning of a story—especially a story written for children of Israel who knew all about Moses, Ezekiel and Isaiah. But it's this claim that makes the timing of John's Gospel so important. It puts us on the edge of our seats from the beginning. When are we going to glimpse the glory of God that John has promised?

When we are told "the hour had come" at the beginning of the farewell sermon in John 13, it's a clue that we're about to see what we've all been waiting for. We're about to glimpse the glory of God. Thirty verses later, after Jesus has washed his disciples' feet and shared the Last Supper with them, he gives the bread to Judas, saying, "This is my body, broken for you." Then, as Judas is leaving to betray him, Jesus says to his disciples, "Now is the Son of Man glorified and God is glorified in him" (John 13:31).

Strange. Why does Jesus think he is glorified when one of his close associates is leaving to get the authorities and blow his whole movement? Why does John, a Jew, think we can see the glory of the "one and only" in this? John seems to be saying that in the moment when Jesus is betrayed and handed over to the executioners, we see the full extent of his love. But how is that?

After three years in a little community of twelve, Jesus shows us what love looks like. Like a household maid, he wraps a towel around his waist and does the job that everyone in the ancient world would pay someone else to do if they could afford it—he washes his disciples' feet. With running water and mass-produced socks, keeping our feet clean has become much easier since biblical times. But we still have dirty work. *Living* in community allows us to know people well enough to see the work they have to do to meet their basic needs. *Loving* in community often looks like choosing to do someone's dirty work for them.

PRAYER OF ST. FRANCIS

Lord, make me an instrument of your peace: where there is hatred let me sow love; where there is injury, pardon; where there is doubt, faith; where there is despair, hope; where there is darknes, light; where there is sadness, joy. Lord, may I not so much seek to be consoled as to console; to be understood as to understand; to be loved as to love. **Because it is in giving that we receive, in pardoning that we are pardoned, in dying that we are born to eternal life: Amen.**

That's the community of Jesus. We are not just about praying for the messy needs of the world in comfortable places
that insulate us from suffering. We are about getting on our
knees and getting our hands dirty in that mess, breaking a
sweat working in the gutters of this world.

Darin and Meeghan grew to love an elderly lady named
Guinn, who they met in the projects of Omaha. Guinn was
afflicted with Alzheimer's and had been left very vulnerable,
without friends or family to care for her. As the government
began to tear down the affordable housing she was living in,
Darin and Meeghan were faced with a difficult question: What
is going to happen to Guinn?

As they prayed and struggled, they tried everything. Darin
and Meeghan worked hard to help Guinn continue to live inde-
pendently as long as possible, as this was her wish. It started
out with simple things, having meals together and doing her
laundry while they talked. It progressed to helping her bathe
at their home, setting up her daily medication, taking her to
appointments and managing her financial affairs.

After a lot of work, it became sadly clear that it was no
longer the best option for Guinn to live on her own anymore. Darin and Meeghan were part of the tough decision
to help her move from independent living to a country nursing home. As Meeghan cleaned out Guinn's apartment, she
came across an old, weathered 3 x 5 card that read "Don't
put me in a nursing home" signed in small print "Guinnev-
ere G. Collins."

Darin and Meeghan began to wrestle with what it meant to
be family to Guinn (who had no kids and never married). Eventually, they became the answer to their own prayers, adopting

Guinn into their own home and family. Now they have lived together for over four years.

It isn't always easy. Guinn's sickness has gotten much worse. She's a wild and eccentric old diva. (She used to be an aspiring actress.) So every moment is an adventure as she tries to remember where she is. Every hour she asks, "Is this the Alps?" "Are we in England?" And sometimes Darin and Meeghan will let her choose her adventure for the day or the hour. They have helped her find ways to continue to paint and make art. And she makes them smile as she tells dirty jokes, looks for her boyfriends and does her little booty-shake-boogie when she gets excited.

A little while back Darin and Meeghan had a child, and now Guinn comes to life as she holds little Justice and brings him into this world. And Darin, Meeghan and Justice will help Guinn make the transition from this world—with a smile on her face and a family around her.

I (Shane) sometimes get accused of seeing the world through rose-colored glasses—only telling the happy stories, not the messy ones. Most of life in the way of Jesus is not that neat. So to keep it real, I must confess that I got a note from Meeghan after she read the story we wrote about her family. I think the story is incomplete without her note.

Shane—

You make us sound nice and gentle when the reality is that loving and caring for Guinn has exposed more ugliness in both of us (mostly me) than I would like to see. It is the craziness of letting myself be vulnerable enough to get this close that I can care so much but be frustrated so profoundly. I hate the disease for her, for me. I don't like wiping poop off of everything every morning. I do it, but it is really hard. So, if you are comfortable (we are), feel free to include some of this ugly struggle so that people in similar spots don't think they are alone or crazy.

Jesus told his community that since he had washed their feet, they should also wash one another's feet. The love that keeps community alive isn't the warm-fuzzy you feel when you're hanging out with friends or the little flutter between your chest and your throat that happens when you meet that special someone (though both of those feelings are nice). The love that makes community is the willingness to do someone else's dirty work.

But that, by itself, is not the glory of God. At least, we don't think that's what John means by "the full extent of his love." Jesus says the Son of Man is glorified when he keeps on loving the one who is forsaking him. The full extent of Jesus' love is washing Judas's feet, serving him dinner and then going to the cross *for him.*

Amber is a massage therapist. She could be making $100 an hour giving massages to rich folks. But she says there are plenty of massage therapists doing that. She lives near to the poor and homeless. She knows plenty of people whose feet are their transportation and is friends with women involved in sex trafficking who walk the red light district all night long. These people have tired, sore feet, and no massage therapist to offer them services, until now. Every week Amber opens her home to them, washes their feet with the most delicate and deliberate touch, and gives them the best foot massages money can't buy.

Sometimes it is easier to wash the feet of prostitutes than it is to wash the feet of the people we live with each day—the people who get on our nerves, don't do their dishes and expect us to pick up on their passive aggression (and certainly *we* don't do any of those things). One of the most radical things we do is love the people we live with, day after day, mistake after mistake. One community we visited had printed T-shirts that read: "Everybody wants a revolution, but nobody wants to do the dishes." It was a constant reminder that the revolution must begin with little acts of love, like washing feet or dishes.

As two people who love both the worldwide church and our particular communities dearly, we have to issue this warning: If you get involved with God's people, you will get hurt. The Holy Spirit makes it possible—compels us, even—to share lives with one another, live together, do each other's dirty work, offer hospitality, make peace, share money, raise kids together, start car co-ops and serve our neighbors. But if you do all those things with broken people (and broken people are the only kind available), you will hurt each other. You will be betrayed in one way or another. And you will, despite your best intentions and greatest hopes, betray. You will even forsake the people who have time and again laid down their lives for you.

But here's the good news: as we have learned to pray "glorify your Son, that your Son may glorify you" in community, we've come to understand a little bit more the truth about God's glory. Truth is, God is not glorified when we try to live together as perfect people. (Communities that strive for perfection are always weeding out the imperfect people—until there's no one left.) Jesus was glorified when he loved the one who would hurt him. He prayed to the Father for strength to love with that kind of love in John 17. Likewise, we are glorified, that God may be glorified, when we keep loving one another, even after we hurt each other. God is glorified when we keep doing the dirty work, even for people who treat us dirty.

That He Might Give Eternal Life

After asking God to glorify the Son, Jesus continues to pray, "you granted him authority over all people that he might give eternal life to all those you have given him" (John 17:2). The One who shows us the glory of God by loving his betrayers also has authority from God to give us eternal life. That's important—especially as we try to live in what Pope John Paul II called a "culture of death." From abortion to the war on terrorism to global warming, the signs of the times say that we are living in a way that is killing us. The uncertainty that this culture produces has most people scared to death. (Have you noticed at airports how they even make little kids take their shoes off at the metal detectors?) What the world needs, more than anything, is eternal life—a way of living that doesn't lead to death but can go on forever. This is the narrow way Jesus speaks of, the one that few find but many are looking for.

Often when Christians talk about "eternal life," we mean life after death. That's not all bad. We're both pretty excited about life after death (though neither one of us is in any rush to get there). But we've been asking together with our communities whether there is life before death. What we're really looking for in our life together and in the church is what the apostle

Paul calls the "life that is truly life" (1 Timothy 6:19). We have to stop promising people life after death when what we are all really asking is if there is life before death. And the good news is—there is. Eternal life begins now. It is living in the presence of God.

It's no accident that Jesus connects eternal life to the glory of God. If God is glorified when people give themselves to each other in love, despite their brokenness and the pain that causes, then God's glory is what you might call "sustainable." Sustainability is a trendy idea in contemporary discussions about how people live. Some have realized, for example, that if there is only so much oil beneath the earth's surface, but almost everything we do on the earth's surface requires oil, then our current way of living cannot be sustained. Likewise, if we produce endless amounts of trash but only have so many places to bury it, that cannot go on and on forever either. So more and more people talk about "sustainable development"—that is, learning to live in a way that we can keep on living without exhausting our resources or drowning ourselves in our own garbage.

The only trouble, of course, is that we can't beat death. We are the masters of keeping people breathing, but we know very little about really being alive. No matter how well we live, life as we know it is a nonrenewable resource. But life as God knows it is renewable. God's life is eternal. It has no beginning. Which also means that it has no end—no future when it will be different than it always has been. So God's life is always here, always now, always with us, always complete.

Jesus shows us "the full extent of his love" John says. And what we see in Jesus is always available to us in God. This is why the Scripture says, "Today is the day of salvation!" It's why Jesus says to the thief on the cross, "Today you will be with me in paradise" (Luke 23:43). It's why Peter says, "With the Lord a day is like a thousand years, and a thousand years are like a day" (2 Peter 3:8). Because the fullness of God's love is always here in the reality that Jesus calls "eternal life."

When Gandhi was traveling on a ship at sea one December, the Christians on board came and asked him if he might deliver a Christmas sermon for them. Having read the Sermon on the Mount every day of his life for decades, Gandhi agreed. He said to those who were gathered to celebrate the birth of the Son of God, "Living Christ means a living cross. Everything else is a living death."

We don't know a better way to summarize what Jesus is praying at the beginning of John 17. To live the glory of God with Jesus is to give ourselves to one another, even as Jesus gave himself for those who betrayed him on the cross. It is a life that, admittedly, looks like dying. But Gandhi is right. Everything else is a living death. To cling to the gift of life we've been given and scramble to protect our own interests is to cooperate in a culture of death that threatens to destroy us all. John 17 begins with a plea for eternal life that will save the world from such death. This is the eternal life that we do not have to die to find. It begins now with a new way of living—and to it there is no end.

5

Praying as a Peculiar People

JESUS' PRAYER FOR UNITY HAS convinced us that learning to love one another is perhaps our most important call. But Jesus goes on to say in John 17:9, "I am not praying for the world, but for those you have given me." Once again, Jesus' words seem strange. Why isn't he praying for the world? We were both raised in good Bible-belt churches, Shane in a Methodist church on the west side of the Appalachians and Jonathan in a Baptist church on the east side of the same range. (We're still trying to figure out this eastside-westside battle that we've heard about since coming to the city, but that's another story.)

In the churches where we grew up, we all memorized John 3:16 long before we went to school: "For God so loved the world, that he gave his only begotten Son, that whosoever believeth in him should not perish, but have everlasting life"

(KJV). That's how much God loves the world—so much that Jesus died for it. So why doesn't Jesus pray for the world in John 17?

Most of the saints who inspire us are people who have cared a lot about God's good world. St. Francis preached to the birds, tamed a vicious wolf, visited with Muslims during the Crusades and sang a canticle to the sun. We have been transformed by God's love through the "worldly" faith of saints like Francis, and we have seen with our own eyes the truth of his conviction. Iraqis and welfare moms, inmates and homeless folk have been our teachers. We have seen the Holy Spirit at work among anarchist punk kids and on military bases, in the marketplace and in the alley. We can say with the songwriter, "This is my Father's world. / He shines in all that's fair."[1] But the longer we press on with the people of God, the more we're learning to see why Jesus says to his Father, "I am not praying for the world."

We have some friends who started a community about twenty years ago in a poor, immigrant neighborhood of San Francisco. At their InterVarsity chapter in college, they had read the over two thousand verses of Scripture about the poor and knew of God's passionate love for the downtrodden and neglected. They wanted to share that love with refugees from Central America, so they moved in together, started a legal clinic in their garage and hosted a summer program for kids in their home. They taught English as a second language (ESL) courses and helped people find jobs. They poured themselves into service because they knew God loved the world and believed that was what they were supposed to be doing.

CANTICLE OF BROTHER SUN
St. Francis of Assisi (1225)

Most high, all-powerful,
all good, Lord!
All praise is yours,
all glory, all honor
And all blessing.

To you alone, Most High,
do they belong.
No mortal lips are worthy
To pronounce your name.

All praise be yours, my Lord,
through all that you have made,
And first my lord Brother Sun,
Who brings the day; and light
you give to us through him.

How beautiful is he, how radiant
in all his splendor!
Of you, Most High,
he bears the likeness.

All praise be yours, my Lord,
through Sister Moon and Stars;
In the heavens you have
made them, bright
And precious and fair.

All praise be yours, My Lord,
through Brothers Wind and Air,
And fair and stormy, all
the weather's moods,
By which you cherish
all that you have made.

All praise be yours, my Lord,
through Sister Water,
So useful, lowly, precious
and pure.

All praise be yours, my Lord,
through Brother Fire,
Through whom you brighten
up the night.
How beautiful is he, how gay!
Full of power and strength.

All praise be yours, my Lord,
through Sister Earth, our mother,
Who feeds us in her sovereignty
and produces
Various fruits with colored
flowers and herbs.

All praise be yours, my Lord,
through those who grant pardon
For love of you; through
those who endure
Sickness and trial.

Happy those who endure
in peace,
By you, Most High,
they will be crowned.

All praise be yours, my Lord,
through Sister Death,
From whose embrace
no mortal can escape.
Woe to those who die
in mortal sin!
Happy those She finds
doing your will!
The second death can
do no harm to them.

Praise and bless my Lord,
and give him thanks,
and serve him with
great humility.

After a number of years, they paused one day to take account of how they were doing. Their service programs were, in some ways, very effective. People had gotten visas, education and jobs. With the money they were earning, they also bought minivans and drove them to their new homes in the suburbs.

But our friends felt conflicted. Many of them had grown up in the suburbs with parents who wanted them to have the very best, but they had decided to move to the city and live in community because they felt a tension between the American Dream and the gospel according to Jesus. If their "ministry" was creating a fast track to the life they'd been called to leave behind, was it really what God wanted from them?

This question led our friends to do some serious thinking about the purpose of the church. Most of them had grown up evangelical and were taught that the purpose of the church is to save people's souls. Their Bible study in college had helped them to see that God offers good news in *this* world—body *and* soul. But somehow their community life had become about meeting people's needs so they could "move on up" in the world; it wasn't so much about giving these people the gospel. They didn't think everyone was supposed to live like them. But neither did they believe an individualistic, other-worldly faith was the answer. So what *is* the gospel, they asked?

Their questions and the Holy Spirit led them to study the book of Ephesians. They noted its extraordinary claims about the church, "which is [Christ's] body, the fullness of him who fills everything in every way" (Ephesians 1:23). They tried to get their minds around that phrase—"the fullness of him who fills everything." What could that mean?

Ephesians seemed to be saying that there was nothing more important in the world than the church. They had seen the terrible power of racism and poverty and violence at work in the lives of immigrant families. But Paul said God's plan was that "now, through the church, the manifold wisdom of God should be made known to the rulers and authorities in the heavenly realms" (Ephesians 3:10). The Bible said the powers and principalities would learn their proper place through the church, living out its purpose in the world. Nothing was more important than the call to be God's peculiar people in the midst of all that was going on in the world.

A lot of intentional communities and justice movements get started because people's hearts are stirred by God's love for the poor and Jesus' passion for justice. In many ways that's our story, and we don't want to belittle what the Holy Spirit is doing in activist communities and justice movements all around the world. But in our own prayer lives, we have learned that activism alone will not sustain community life, and protest doesn't necessarily make us more loving people. It is so very important for the church to learn to name the powers and principalities, and to cry out against them. But it is equally important for us to remember that God has a plan to save the whole world through this peculiar people called "church." So nothing is more important than figuring out how to be church together.

This is a hard thing to grasp, but we think it's true: Jesus chooses not to pray for the world *because he wants to save the world*. The reason we are not to be *of* the world is so we may be *for* the world. As our brother Rodney Clapp says so well, we are still to "eavesdrop on the world" even as we create a new one, and practice the art of selective engagement and sanctified subversion.[2] We are cultural refugees. The beautiful monastics of renewal throughout church history were cultural refugees. They ran to the desert not to flee from the world but to save the world—from itself.

That They May Be One

Since Jesus knows that God's plan is to save the world through a people, he prays first for us who've been adopted into God's family, begging the Father that "they may be one as we are one" (John 17:22). Jesus prays that the church would be unified by the strange kind of love we talked about in chapter four. While we are eager to ask what we can do for the world (justice and advocacy work is so important), Jesus is more concerned with who we are in the world. He wants us to pledge our allegiance, before anything else, to the church.

Jesus doesn't just want to teach us a new kind of love. Praying with him in John 17, we also learn a new kind of politics. Though it's often hard for us to see, our imaginations are held captive by the political options that the world offers. We have learned this by listening to debates about poverty, an issue that has a huge impact on our neighborhoods. Conservatives—or people on the political right—say that the best way to reduce poverty in a capitalist economy is to encourage business with tax breaks and thereby create more jobs. Liberals—or people on the political left—insist that the answer is to use more tax money to fund government programs that both address people's basic needs and alleviate the causes of poverty.

People argue a lot about the differences between these two camps. We're not sure who's right, but we have noticed that the debate doesn't seem to do much for people in our neighborhoods. What it does, unfortunately, is divide the church. Christians seem to feel more allegiance to the positions of the political left or the right than we feel to God's people. Rather than share what we have in common so that no one has a need, we self-segregate into conservative and liberal congregations or black and white congregations or upper- and lower-class congregations. The powers and principalities think themselves wise. And the wisdom of God seems like foolishness.

But thankfully, some holy fools keep joining with Jesus to pray that we will be one as the Father and the Son are one.

About twenty years ago there was a little congregation of about four hundred folks that didn't have a ton of money, and the pastor didn't have health coverage. He had an accident, and the congregation decided to pool their money to cover his medical bills. It all worked out so well that the pastor ended up saying, "If you can do that for me, we can do that for each other." So they did. They created a common fund to cover medical bills that arose.

Now we are part of that community, which has grown to over twenty thousand people.[3] Every month we get a newsletter that tells who is in the hospital, and how to pray for them. And we know that our money is going directly to meet the needs of brothers and sisters. Over the twenty years, this group has met over $400 million in medical bills. What a beautiful embodiment of a political alternative. And we may not even all agree on the political issue of "health care," but we can agree on the political embodiment of hope—that we should be taking care of each other, especially the most vulnerable among us. And that makes our good news contagious and tangible.

I Have Sent Them into the World

There is a danger in being a peculiar people, especially if we have the privilege of choosing (some of us are peculiar without trying, you know). Things can begin to look pretty separatist and insular when the people of God becomes the organizing principle for our lives. The Amish, for example, are serious about taking care of each other in their communities. But they are also often accused of trying to get away from the world to create their own space, just for them. This criticism, whether it is valid or not, raises an important question: what does it mean for a peculiar people to be sent into the world, as Christ was sent into the world?

After teaching us what God's love looks like and redefining our politics, Jesus' prayer shows us something important about mission. "As you sent me into the world," Jesus prays to the Father, "I have sent them into the world" (John 17:18). We are sent into the world as Jesus was.

I (Jonathan) grew up in a Southern Baptist church that cared a lot about missions. We were proud of the fact that our denomination had the largest missions organization in the world. I learned to quote Jesus' charge to his disciples in the King James English: "Go ye therefore, and teach all nations" (Matthew 28:19). Without a doubt, I knew that I was sent. So when I was sixteen years old I went to Zimbabwe and rode through the bush on a dirt bike, showing the *Jesus* film with a gas-powered generator and a reel-to-reel projector.

When our little team rode into a village, people would run to follow our dirt bikes. We circled them up, cranked the generator and hung an electric light bulb in the tree, shining as a beacon in the night to draw people in. We would sing and talk with people until a large crowd gathered, then we would show the film about Jesus' life, give an altar call at the end and pray with people who wanted to invite Jesus into their hearts.

I will never forget the night when I was up front beckoning people to come, and a woman came forward with her baby, asking me to bless him. She did not seem terribly impressed with the story about Jesus, but she *really* wanted me to bless her baby. I had one of those experiences where you see yourself from the outside, imagining what you must look like to someone else. Here I was, a tall white kid among black Ndebele people, proclaiming with my dirt-bike arrival the miraculous power of gasoline, electricity and video technology.

This woman wanted me to bless her baby because she thought I was blessed—the embodiment of everything that development and education promised her child. My head was swimming and I felt my knees wobble. I stammered something, leading the woman to another member of our evangelistic team, and then excused myself to some dark corner, beyond the reach of our sixty-watt bulb.

The only way I can describe that feeling is that it was something like being hit in the gut. What it produced was a lack of confidence that we see abounding in our generation of evangelicals (or "postevangelicals," as some say). A growing awareness of how Christian missions has been tied to colonialism, nation-state violence and global economic trade has caused many American Christians to wonder whether evangelism is even a good idea. Maybe we should just do relief and development. Maybe we should focus more on interreligious dialogue.

But Jesus still prays to the Father, "as you sent me into the world, I have sent them." So maybe the problem isn't *that* the church does missions in the world but *how* we've done it. If it's true that the church hasn't, for the most part, been a peculiar people in America, then it makes sense that we may have missed the mark when it comes to evangelism. But that's no reason to give up on evangelism. Jesus prays that we would go as he was sent. What we need, more than anything, is to pay attention to how Jesus came into the world.

A lot of good New Testament scholarship in recent decades has paid close attention to the fact that Jesus came into the world *as a Jew*. Matthew's Gospel seems to highlight this. He starts his story of Jesus' life with a genealogy that goes on long enough for most of our eyes to glaze over and skim a little. Maybe Matthew knew that, because he offers a little summary at the end: "Thus there were fourteen generations in all from Abraham to David, fourteen from David to the exile to Babylon, and fourteen from the exile to the Messiah" (Matthew 1:17). Just in case you forgot to count, Matthew wants to point out that God has a plan and that it's unfolding like clockwork. The history of God's people all leads up to the life of this one Jew, Jesus Christ.

Matthew goes on to make his point by emphasizing the similarities between Jesus' life and the history of Israel. Just like the Hebrew children were killed by Pharaoh, the children in Bethlehem are killed by Herod when Jesus is born. And just as Joseph and all Israel with him had to flee into Egypt to survive, so too does Jesus go to Egypt to wait out the reign of Herod. Like Israel, Jesus passes through the waters in baptism and wanders in the wilderness (in his case, only forty days). He emerges to call twelve disciples, like the twelve tribes of Israel. And when Jesus begins to teach the law in Matthew 5, he goes up on a mountain. Anyone remember a story about the law coming down from a mountain?

So Jesus came into the world as a Jew, retelling the story of God's people in his own body. In his sermon on that mountainside, Jesus says to the people of Israel, "Do not think that I have come to abolish the Law or the Prophets; I have not come to abolish them but to fulfill them" (Matthew 5:17). Evidently the Pharisees and other temple authorities down in Jerusalem did not get a transcript of this sermon. Because this is exactly what they accuse Jesus of—disregarding the laws of Israel and blaspheming their God. Jesus came as a Jew to Israel, but his interpretation of what it means to live as God's people in the world is so surprising that the people in charge of the temple have him killed.

What is so radically different about Jesus' approach to being God's people? Maybe it is his insistence that God has enough love to include everyone. Most of the fights Jesus gets into are about him hanging out with the wrong crowd or healing social outcasts or saying that the temple was supposed to be a place "for all nations" (Mark 11:17). In Greek, the word that we translate "nation" also means "Gentile"—that is, not a Jew. From the poor Canaanite woman to the occupying force's centurion, Jesus always seems to be whispering, "There's room for one more at my Father's table." By becoming Israel, Jesus shows us what it means to be a blessing to the nations. Ultimately, it looks like going to the cross, pouring out the blood of his people for the sake of the world.

Life in community has given us frequent opportunity to think about what it means to trust that there's always enough for one more. Enough food for one more hungry kid at the table. Enough space for one more person who needs a bed for the night. Enough time for one more addict who wants to try to kick the habit. Enough patience to listen to a brother's

Hail, O cross! I have come to thee whom I know to be mine; I have come to thee because thou longest for me. I know thy mystery for the sake of which thou art set up. Thou art fastened to the world to make firm what is unstable. In one direction thou reachest up into heaven to witness to the Spirit above. In the other direction thou art spread out to the right and to the left that thou mayest put to flight the dreadful hostile power and draw the world into one. In a third direction thou art planted in the earth in order to join all that is on the earth and under the earth to the things that are in heaven.

O cross, tool of salvation of the most high! O cross, banner of Christ's victory over all enemies! O cross, planted upon the earth and bearing fruit in heaven! O name of the cross, that containest the universe!

Well done, O cross, that hast bound the whole circumference of the world! Well done, O shape full of clarity, that hast given shape to thine own unshapely outward appearance! Hail to the invisible chastisement with which thou strikest at the very nature of the many gods and drivest out from this humankind him who invited them! Well done, O cross, that hast cast off the ruler, brought home the robber, and called the apostle to repentance, and hast not thought it beneath thy dignity to accept us.

But how long am I speaking instead of letting myself be embraced by the cross in order that in the cross I may be awakened to life! Through the cross I go into the death common to all, and depart from life.

Acts of Andrew **(Andrew's Death)**

concern one more time. Enough grace to make it through one more hard meeting. We have not always trusted that there was enough. Our communities, like all Christian households, have failed to depend on the unlimited overflow of God's economy. But we have seen enough to believe that it's true— and to want to believe, even when we doubt.

In his book *The Rise of Christianity*, sociologist Rodney Stark asks how faith in Jesus spread from a little community on the margins of the Roman Empire to the whole known world over the course of just a few centuries. He doesn't ask the question as a missiologist, but his observations are fascinating as we think about missions.

As far as Stark can tell, employing the tools of sociology and history, Christianity spread throughout the world because communities of Jesus' followers were willing to welcome outcasts and care for the dying, even at the risk of their own lives. In the ancient world, before modern medicine made abortions possible, people who had unwanted children would leave babies outside of the city to die from exposure and be eaten by wild animals. But early Christian communities, because they believed every life was a gift from God, would rescue these children from abandonment and raise them as their own. Evidently, a majority of these kids were girls. They grew up to be Christian women who had children of their own, and they passed their faith on to their children.

Another way early Christianity grew, Stark says, was through Christians' care for the dying. Because there was no way to stop the spread of plagues in the ancient world, it was common practice to flee the city when a plague broke out, leaving the sick and dying behind. Stark says that the Christians, instead of running for their lives, would stay to take care of those who were suffering the plague. Often all that people needed to survive the flu or other viruses was the basic nursing care of food, water and a bath. Meanwhile, Christian nurses were developing immunity to these sicknesses. Stark guesses that when the patients who had been given up for dead recovered, they were interested to hear about the faith of those who had stayed around to save them. And when the plagues came around again, more Christians had the immunity to survive.[4]

Maybe Christians wouldn't be nearly as embarrassed about evangelism if we tried sharing good news more like the early church did. Our friends with a group called InnerChange like to say that "it takes a community to reach a community." For the past twenty-five years they have been planting little communities of Christians who want to love one another and their neighbors in slum communities around the world. Our friends Phileena and Chris Heuertz, after spending time with Mother Teresa, had a similar vision for a new kind of mission and organized a comunity called Word Made Flesh (WMF). They don't just invite people to accept Jesus as their personal Savior, and they don't just do relief work, though they do some of all this in their life together. What groups like InnerChange and WMF are experimenting with is the idea of being God's people together, on mission in the world. That they are questioning traditional boundaries and old rules gives us hope that they can help all of us see how to go into the world as Jesus was sent.[5]

Before the two of us went to Iraq at the beginning of the U.S. occupation there, we met for breakfast at a little diner in North Philadelphia. We talked for a couple of hours, but one question seemed to be at the heart of our conversation: why is

God leading us to do this? One of the ironies we noted about the whole situation was that many evangelical churches that are passionate about sharing the good news of Jesus with all people were equally passionate about bombing Baghdad and eliminating Saddam Hussein. It seemed to us that we had to go be with Iraqis if for no other reason than to show them by our presence that not all Christians wanted to bomb them. How else would they ever believe the gospel message?

Since we were both living in Philadelphia at the time, a reporter named Jim O'Neil, from the *Philadelphia Inquirer,* heard about our trip as Christian peacemakers and asked for an interview before we left. While we were gone, we put Jim on our email update list, and he wrote a couple of articles based on our reports. When we returned from the Middle East, Jim called us up and said he wanted to share a letter he had received in response to one of his articles about our peacemaking mission.

The letter was from a woman living in the Philadelphia area. "When I heard George W. Bush say that he was an evangelical Christian," she wrote, "I vowed to myself that I could never be one. But when I read your story, I thought, 'Maybe I should think again about Jesus and Christianity.' "

Before going to Iraq as Christian peacemakers, we thought we had to trust God and go for the sake of the gospel in the Middle East. And maybe that was true in some small way. But we also learned that the credibility of the gospel right here in America was at stake. And it always is. Jesus prays at the end of John 17 for "those who will believe"—for all God's family, including us—that we may be in the Father as the Father was in Jesus "so that the world may believe" (v. 20).

A lot of people we talk to are concerned about the renewal of the church for one reason or another. Some worry that old forms of congregational life are irrelevant and need to be revived. Others feel as if the language they were given to talk about God rings hollow and lacks meaning. Many people look at the empty cathedrals in Europe and wonder if our mega-churches will become museums in the next generation.

While we share these concerns, we also don't want to worry too much about "how to save the church in America." We don't want our love for the church to turn into one more way that the world convinces us to live in fear of death. Yes, parts of the church are always dying. But what really excites us is the way our God stirs up the ruins, always eager to give new life. The world will not believe that the gospel is true because we struggle hard enough to save a sinking ship. The world will believe when we practice resurrection where we are because we know the joy of new life.

Yes, they will know we are Christians by our love. And it is when we become one as God is one that the world is able to be fascinated by God's love and grace that can reconcile even enemies. I (Shane) have a friend in Africa who is from a nomadic tribe that had no home and very few possessions, but he says that they had community. In fact he goes on to say that one of the greatest hindrances to the spreading of the gospel among his people was that Christians talked about reconciliation and unity, but the church was very fractured and had little integrity. He reminds me of the words of one pastor I heard, "We better get it together because Jesus is coming back, and he coming for a Bride, not a harem." Sometimes when people ask how many people live in our community houses, we reply: "On good days, one."

Journalists sometimes try to get a certain position statement from "the new monastics" or from our communities on hot-button issues. Thankfully, there are plenty of beliefs and practices that we can say assuredly are common marks of our discipleship.[6] But then there are those that are much trickier, much more complex when dealing with people and with Scripture. For instance, the question "Where do you stand on the homosexuality issue?" often comes up. One thing we are proud of is that we have communities where people do not see the same on every issue, and yet we are able to live together, work through that and learn from each other. One of the greatest witnesses of the church can be our ability to disagree well. The world has not seen many folks who can do that.

As we go deeper with Jesus into the prayer of John 17, love and unity among God's people is our growing passion. The world needs peculiar people who live the distinctive way of Jesus. But if we are so radical that we fail to love one another in our pursuit of that way, then we are to be pitied more than the heretics. Walking in Jesus' way and growing in love for one another requires discernment. To do that well, we have to grow in wisdom by the Spirit's power. Thankfully, we have another prayer from Ephesians to help guide our growth like a trellis.

EPHESIANS 1:15-23

Part Three

Ever since I heard about your faith in the Lord Jesus and your love for all his people, I have not stopped giving thanks for you, remembering you in my prayers. I keep asking that the God of our Lord Jesus Christ, the glorious Father, may give you the Spirit of wisdom and revelation, so that you may know him better. I pray that the eyes of your heart may be enlightened in order that you may know the hope to which he has called you, the riches of his glorious inheritance in his people, and his incomparably great power for us who believe. That power is the same as the mighty strength he exerted when he raised Christ from the dead and seated him at his right hand in the heavenly realms, far above all rule and authority, power and dominion, and every name that can be invoked, not only in the present age but also in the one to come. And God placed all things under his feet and appointed him to be head over everything for the church, which is his body, the fullness of him who fills everything in every way.

6

Growing Deeper in Spiritual Wisdom

THERE'S A STORY FROM THE DESERT mothers and fathers that we want to tell, even though we don't entirely understand it. It comes from a time in the fourth century when lots of people found it convenient to call themselves Christian but the faith seemed to make less and less of a difference in people's lives. In those days some women and men heard a call to go out into the desert and learn to pray. Without planning to start anything, they became the ammas and abbas of the first monastic movement in the church.

The story is told of an Abba Lot who went to visit Abba Joseph, an older and wiser monk. He explained to him what he had been doing to know God better. "As far as I can, I say my little office, I fast a little, I pray and meditate, I live in peace as far as I can, I purify my thoughts. What else can I do?"

It was a sincere question. Abba Lot was wrestling with something all of us have to face if we want to pray. Sometimes, after you have done everything you know to do, there's still a sense that something is missing—still a longing for more.

"What else can I do?" Abba Lot asked. Without saying anything, Abba Joseph stood up and stretched his hands toward heaven. From what Abba Lot could see, the tips of Abba Joseph's fingers were on fire, flickering in the wind like ten candle flames. As Abba Joseph stood there, his hands glowing like a burning bush, he said to Abba Lot, "If you will, you can become all flame."[1]

I Keep Asking . . .

Like we said, we're not sure we understand this story. We want to be mystics, but we still have a long way to go. One wannabe monk said, "I really want to be a monk, but don't have the will. So right now I am a monk on Mondays and Wednesdays." Sometimes that's where we find ourselves. But something about the Abba's story feels compelling. And it reminds us of the prayer in Ephesians 1:15-17: "Ever since I heard about your faith in the Lord Jesus and your love for all his people, I have not stopped giving thanks for you, remembering you in my prayers. I keep asking . . ."

Faith in Jesus and love for all the saints are pretty important things. As the old saying goes, "If the saints stopped praying, the world would fall apart." You could say that the Lord's Prayer is about faith in Jesus—what it means to trust God's vision for a whole new way of life. And Jesus' prayer in John 17 is about love for one another in Christ's body, the church.

A whole lot of prayer is about learning to trust Jesus and love our sisters and brothers.

But Abba Joseph and Ephesians 1 both seem to say that's not all prayer is about. In this prayer for the Ephesians, Paul gives thanks for their faith and love, but he also says, "I keep asking that the God of our Lord Jesus Christ, the glorious Father, may give you the Spirit of wisdom and revelation, so that you may know him better" (1:17). Even as he celebrates a healthy community that is grounded in Christ, Paul keeps begging God that they—and we—would know the "what else" of the Christian life.

One of my (Shane's) mentors is a Catholic monk, and he is always telling me to keep myself surrounded by people who make me shine brighter for God. True spiritual community is about surrounding ourselves with people who look like the person we want to become. We live in close proximity to people who closely resemble the character of Jesus, and they rub off on us.

As you can tell, we are both pretty proud of our Southern heritage (okay, *some* of our Southern heritage). In the South we have a saying: "You are the spittin' image of" someone. It's shorthand for being so much like someone they could have spit you out of their mouth—spittin' image (go ahead, try it out. It won't hurt). It means more than just "you look like them." It goes beyond just appearance and into character and temperament. It means that you remind people of that person. You have their charisma. You do the same things they did.

In the truest sense Christians are to be the spittin' image of Jesus in the world. We are to be the things he was. We are to preach the things he preached and live the things he lived. We are to follow in the footsteps of our rabbi so closely that we get his dust on us. We are to remind the world of Jesus. That's what's so exciting about being part of the church. In the saints we can see our own potential to radiate God's love.

I (Jonathan) love to visit some monks I've gotten to know at a Benedictine monastery in rural Minnesota. For 1,500 years Benedictines have been praying the liturgy of the hours, taking care of one another, practicing hospitality and trying to know God better. As an order, Benedictines have stocked up some spiritual wisdom. At this particular community, like most communities in the United States, many of the brothers are also quite old themselves. Some of them have been on an intensive journey of spiritual formation now for fifty, sixty or seventy years.

> *Let us get up then, at long last, for the Scriptures rouse us when they say: It is high time for us to arise from sleep. Let us open our eyes to the light that comes from God, and our ears to the voice from heaven that every day calls out this charge: If you hear his voice today, do not harden your hearts.*
>
> **Rule of St. Benedict**

Brother Angelo is 106. When he turned 100, the brothers threw a big birthday party for him. While they were eating cake and swapping stories, a younger brother (by young, I mean in his sixties) said he was moved to ask Brother Angelo about his journey with God. Here was Brother Angelo, an elder brother who had been a monk for nearly eighty years. He had fought the good fight. He had stayed the course. His younger brother wondered if Angelo felt like he had in some sense "arrived" after so many years.

"Brother Angelo," he asked, "you've been a monk for a long time. Do you feel like you've got it figured out?" Brother Angelo was silent for what seemed like a long time, and the younger brother started to feel a little awkward. Had Angelo not heard him? Had he asked a stupid question? Finally, Angelo leaned forward and, looking off into the distance, whispered in his raspy voice, "Oh no . . . there is still so much to learn."

When it comes to prayer, there is always still so much to learn. The journey to God is not like a trip to St. Louis. We both travel a good bit, visiting colleges, churches and communities around the country. There are faster and slower ways to travel. You can walk or you can bike or you can ride a veggie-powered car (all of which we highly recommend). If you're in a hurry, you can take a train or plane (which we sometimes do too). But if you're going to St. Louis, it's always more or less the same. You set out from where you are and move closer and closer toward your destination until, finally, you arrive.

That's how a trip to St. Louis goes. But it's not the same with our journey toward God. Because God is not a finite place in Missouri. God is infinite in goodness and everywhere in glory. Which is to say, God is not like us. We are limited creatures on a journey into our limitless Creator. "Our hearts are restless until they find rest in Thee," St. Augustine prayed.

But rest in God is not stagnant. We don't sit still on the banks of

> *I sought pleasure, nobility, and truth not in God but in the beings He had created, myself, and others. Thus I fell into sorrow and confusion and error. Thanks be to Thee, my Joy and my Glory and my Hope and my God: thanks be to Thee for Thy gifts: but do Thou preserve them in me. Thus thou wilt preserve me, and the things Thou hast given me will increase and be made perfect, and I shall be with Thee: because even that I exist is Thy gift.*
>
> **St. Augustine, *Confessions***

the Mississippi and gaze at God like we might admire that big arch they have in St. Louis. No, the rest of God is a dance to a never-ending hymn. We call it "eternal life" because it goes on and on forever. The One we are chasing after has already found us, but that only makes us eager to know God more. There's still so much to learn, Brother Angelo whispers. If you want, Abba Joseph says with a nod toward the inexpressible mystery of God, you can become all flame.

It was once said that Francis of Assisi had such a fire in his eyes that one of his brothers told him: "You are on fire my friend, you had better put yourself out or you are going to burn up the world." And Francis replied, "My brother, God is a consuming fire. We must burn with God or else we will be consumed by the fire."

Beyond faith in Jesus and love for one another, Ephesians 1 teaches us to pray for spiritual wisdom. Proverbs says that the gray hair of the old is an honor because it is a sign of wisdom. Most people with gray hair have been around the block a time or two. They've seen some stuff and tried some things. Years of experience and reflection have given them wisdom. And that's important. But *spiritual* wisdom is something more than the know-how you gain if you just keep on living. Spiritual wisdom is the fruit of a consistent walk into God's never-ending glory.

One of the early fathers of the church, Gregory of Nyssa, said, "The contemplation of God's face is the unending journey accomplished by following directly behind the Word."[2] That is spiritual wisdom—what you begin to see after two or twenty or a hundred years of following directly behind Jesus. And that is what this prayer in Ephesians 1 is about—growing deeper in the eternal wisdom of God.

The Hope to Which He Has Called You

Paul prays that "the eyes of your heart may be enlightened in order that you may know the hope to which he has called you" (Ephesians 1:18). We've already talked about the way of life God calls us into—the politics, economics and social vision of God's kingdom. We've considered what it means that God has called us to be a people. So we've talked a good talk about the substance of God's calling.

People who believe in Jesus are usually pretty interested in what God calls us to do and to be in the world. (This is why books on "God's purpose for your life" sell so well.) But Paul keeps praying that we would know the *hope* to which we've been called. Hope, evidently, is part of the "what else" God wants to give us. It's good for us to see God's vision for our lives. And it's good to tell other people about God's dream for the world. It is an excellent thing to begin living into God's vision for the kingdom.

But even if we are doing all of this, God still wants to give us more. "I want you to share my hope," the Spirit whispers in this prayer. The Spirit doesn't just want us to hear God's call and obey. That's not enough. There's still more, Ephesians says. We can learn to share God's hope as we grow in spiritual wisdom.

We are members of young communities and spend time with lots of other communities, college fellowships and new churches around the country. Most of the young people we spend time with need encouragement more than anything else. This isn't always easy to see at first. Often young people have a lot of energy and pour themselves into projects with incredible passion. They feed the hungry, welcome strangers, organize their neighborhoods, advocate for marginalized people, build houses, plant gardens, take care of children and get in the way of violence. What is more, there are almost always a handful of people in any young community or church reading books, taking courses and reflecting critically on the world they live in. Around dinner tables and in family meetings they talk theology and sociology, urban and family planning theories. Often these young communities abound with vitality, combining good ideas with faithful practice.

But almost always, when we listen to our young brothers and sisters, they express doubts and fears about their ability to sustain what they have started. What do you do when the novelty wears off? What happens when kids start growing up and parents lose their adrenaline? Is the kingdom just an ideal that young people flirt with, or has God called us into something that we can commit ourselves to for the long haul—after the honeymoon euphoria begins to fade a little and we see each other's flaws, smell each other's farts and stumble in our own frailty?

Ephesians beckons us to grow in spiritual wisdom so we can begin to share divine hope. And God's hope is what we all need to stick with Jesus for the long haul. God's hope is Abraham, all alone out under the stars. He is old and without a child. But God's hope still says, "All peoples on earth will be blessed through you" (Genesis 12:3). God's hope is Ruth, a "Moabitess" outsider to the chosen people, her husband buried in the ground, saying to her mother-in-law, "Your people will be my people and your God my God" (Ruth 1:16). God's hope is Israel standing out in the desert with the Red Sea in front of them and Pharaoh's army at their back. God's hope says, "The LORD will fight for you; you need only to be still" (Exodus 14:14).

You can't really learn God's hope like you learn the logic of an argument or the details of a story. It's more like learning to belly laugh. You catch hope from someone who has it down in their gut. We can't tell you how to trust God in the midnight hour, when all of your strength is spent and you can't see any way out of the troubles that you and your community face. And it seems that even Jeremiah or Mother Teresa don't have an answer for how to feel near to God all the time. But we can surround ourselves with people who have fed us hope.

John Perkins is one of our mentors who has helped us learn God's hope. John Perkins is a visionary leader from the Civil Rights days, who knows well the brutality humans are capable of. He grew up as a sharecropper in the 1940s and spent much of his life watching his friends be abused by white folks. Police officers killed his brother Clyde, and yet John's life radiates hope. We've heard one fellow share how he told John about his racist grandmother, and after listening intently, John said: "Does your grandmother like blueberries? Let's go visit her." And they did, fully armed with a bowl of berries.

There is no doubt we need justice to roll down like water. And yet justice without grace still leaves us thirsty. Justice without reconciliation falls short of the gospel of Jesus. Love fills in the gaps of justice. John has lived for us what it looks like when justice and reconciliation kiss (Psalm 85:10). John Perkins did not just call for an end to the hate crimes of the KKK, but he became friends with a reborn Klansman. He is one of those people who reminds us that we are better than the worst things we do.

Because white congregations in America have so often intellectualized faith and individualized our relationship with God, people who are hungry for community and drawn to justice movements are usually white. So we find ourselves trying to learn how to be the people of God with other white folks a lot of the time. The trouble with this isn't just that we end up reproducing communities marked by racial division (though this is something that troubles us deeply). We also continue to suffer the deficiencies of white theology.

White folks are big on ideas, and we try hard to put our ideas into practice. But ideas are not what sustains us when times get hard. In our experience, it wasn't until we encountered the spiritual wisdom that black churches and charismatic Christianity possess in abundance that hope really came alive. We have much to learn from people who know struggle.

Two of the oldest intentional Christian communities in the United States—Koinonia Farm in Americus, Georgia, and Reba Place Fellowship in Evanston, Illinois—testify to this need. At different times in their histories, both of these communities have focused on charismatic renewal, learning from black members and trusting the pastoral leadership of people who have more spiritual wisdom than academic degrees.

Both of our communities have been sustained by the black and Latino congregations in our neighborhoods. In the midst of difficult discernment, when we're not sure what to do about something that seems so important, it's good to be able to worship with people who know how to sing, "He may not come when you want him / But he's always right on time / He's an on-time God / Yes, he is."

In Durham, I (Jonathan) studied theology at Duke Divinity School. I got a good education there, for which I'm grateful, but after I graduated I knew I still had a lot to learn. So I asked Ann Atwater if she would take me on as her student. Ann is a black woman in her seventies who grew up the daughter of sharecroppers in rural North Carolina. She memorized Scripture at her father's knee and somewhere along the way absorbed the songs of the black church.

When Ann was a young woman, she came to Durham and took a job cleaning white folks' houses for thirty cents an hour. She says she walked to and from work to save the dime she would have spent on the bus. Her husband left her, and Ann struggled to put food on the table for herself and her two daughters. But somehow, God provided. There was always something to eat.

When the Civil Rights movement hit Durham, some local organizers met Ann and learned that she could talk. She quickly became an organizer herself and led the local movement. "Back then we had to holler to be heard," Ann says. She hollered in the streets and hollered at city council meetings. When Ann hollered at C. P. Ellis, head of the Ku Klux Klan in Durham, she said she wanted to cut his head off.

But one day Ann got a call asking if she would cochair the committee to integrate Durham County Schools, together with C. P. Ellis. "I ain't working with that cracker!" Ann said, slamming down the phone. But then she thought about how the paper would say she was scared to work with a white man. So she called back and said, "I'd be happy to cochair that committee."

What happened between Ann and C. P. can only be described as a miracle. They went into ten days of intensive meetings as enemies who refused to talk to one another. In the course of their work, however, they heard how their children were sharing the same struggles in school. Somehow, the dividing wall between them disintegrated. They became friends and committed to work together for the good of their communities. "Look what the Lord can do," Ann likes to say when she tells her story. "He'll turn things around just like that!"

Ann has been infected with God's hope for the world. She knows that things don't have to stay the way they are if they're not the way God made them to be. "I'm tired!" she'll say sometimes when she's begging for money to rebuild her community center or for housing for a friend who's homeless. "I'm tired" doesn't mean "I'm about to give up" for Ann. "I'm tired" means you better do something to help me.

I'm amazed by the persuasive power of Ann's hope. This is a hope that is learned and inherited, not one that we can get from books alone. It's no wonder that Paul writes in another letter to the young Timothy: "I am reminded of your sincere faith, which first lived in your grandmother Lois and in your mother Eunice and, I am persuaded, now lives in you" (2 Timothy 1:5).

We are grateful for the faith that has lived in our spiritual mothers and fathers and has been passed on to us. It's worth pausing for a minute to think of their names—the living ones and dead ones, the famous ones and the infamous ones. Thanks be to God.

7

Receiving Our Inheritance

SPIRITUAL WISDOM IS ABOUT GROWING DEEPER in hope. But Paul doesn't just pray that we would know the hope that we've been called to. He also asks God to help us see "the riches of his glorious inheritance in his people" (Ephesians 1:18). Beyond a hope to keep us going, God also wants to give us an inheritance. As soon as Paul prays for us to feel God's hope deep down inside of us, he asks that we would also know it isn't an empty hope. "Hope is a thing with feathers," Emily Dickinson wrote, offering a nice image for the uplifting nature of hope. But things with feathers also tend to float above the ground most of the time.

Spirituality can be like that. We can't write about prayer without engaging the spiritual wisdom and practices that have been so important to saints—God's people—in every genera-tion. But spiritual language is dangerous. Talk about "hope" can easily lead to obsession with self-fulfillment and our own feelings. "Spiritual wisdom" can devolve into watered-down self-help if it is not anchored in something as concrete as an inheritance.

As we remember the saints and think about the character of Christ, we begin to have the things that they were become a part of who we are. I (Shane) spend a lot of time thinking about the fruit of the Spirit—love, joy, peace, patience, kindness, gentleness, goodness, faithfulness and self-control. In fact, I painted them on big boards and hung them from the windows of our row house in North Philly, hoping those fruits would take root in our neighborhood. We have them painted on our walls, so that we "think on these things" that remind us of God. And then they become a part of us.

In the early days of The Simple Way, we had a young woman from Brazil named Lydia living in the community. She was petite and, like many of the women in our community, she was a fireball: sassy, bold, somehow able to be both gentle and direct.

One day when Lydia was traveling on the train, a fellow sat down next to her and pulled a knife. "Listen carefully," he said, "Here's what's gonna happen. You are going to hand me your bag, get off at the next station, and not say a word."

Lydia looked at the man directly. "My name is Lydia," she said winsomely, unflinchingly, "and I am from Brazil."

The man stared blankly, taken aback. Lydia continued, "My bag is filled with photos and addresses of my family, and those mean a lot to me but will do you no good. I'd imagine what you want is money. There is no money in my bag. However, I have some money in my pocket, so here's what we'll do. I'll get out my money, give you $20, you get off at the next station, and we won't say a word."

At the next stop, the man did just what Lydia had told him to. It takes time to digest the fruits of the Spirit to the point that they are part of us.

I spoke at a congregation not long ago where a young man was headed to Iraq as a soldier. After my sermon on peacemaking, the pastor spontaneously asked me to pray for the man. What was I to pray? I prayed the fruits of the Spirit slowly, naming them one by one, and asked that God would help those things to live in him.

The young recruit came up to me afterward with tears in his eyes and said that is exactly what he needed to hear, because those were not things being instilled in him in the army. I told him if he felt like the fruits in him could not survive, to let us know and we would help him get out of the military.

What is this "inheritance in his people" that Paul is asking God to help us see? In Ephesians 1:14, just before this prayer, Paul says that the Holy Spirit is God's down payment, guaranteeing our inheritance until the redemption of those who are God's possession—namely, the church. This seems to say that God has already given us some of what he is going to give us completely.

In business they call this earnest money. If you're serious about buying a house, for example, the bank will want you to put 10 percent down so that they know you're serious about paying the rest back. Ephesians says that the Holy Spirit is something like earnest money on our inheritance. But here's where the analogy breaks down. Because money can be divided up pretty easily: x number of dollars now, x number later. But how can you divide up God?

Paul says we have the Holy Spirit now—the Spirit who is completely God. God's presence with us now in the person of the Holy Spirit is earnest money on God's presence with us for eternity. But when God tries to merely give a deposit, you end up getting more than everything at once. Because God always says, "I give you myself." And there's no such thing as 10 percent of God. The deposit is the total package—and God just keeps on giving, like an ever-flowing stream. This is why Jesus always says, "The kingdom of God is coming and has now come." If we are ready to believe it, what will be in the end is already available to us now in the gift of the Holy Spirit.

It's not surprising that the Pentecostal movement in America grew out of poor and marginalized communities where people heard about "the riches of his glorious inheritance in his people" and knew that was good news for them. People with economic and social power aren't usually very interested in the Holy Spirit. Often, people who "talk proper" are afraid of this mysterious member of the holy Trinity. *Father* and *Son* are words we understand, even if we don't usually start them with a capital letter. But spirits don't often slip into polite conversation (except in liquid form, when sipped from a martini glass). Whatever the Holy Spirit is, it's not the sort of thing you'd talk about at a cocktail party.

But throughout the history of the church, the Holy Spirit has been important to people on the margins. And those are the people the church has called "saints." Jesus didn't draft the first disciples from the best and brightest of the students at the temple, but from fishing boats, tax booths and radical religious movements, folks with nothing to lose and everything in the world to hope for. The Holy Spirit came on this motley crew in Jerusalem, and they went around saying they had a message everyone needed to hear.

The martyrs in the first few centuries of the church came from all classes of society. But they were, across the board, people who were crazy enough to say that the Spirit within them had more authority than the soldier in front of them. In the fourth and fifth centuries, when monasticism was born in the Egyptian desert, it wasn't ecclesiastical power brokers who led the movement. It was, instead, laypeople—many of them uneducated peasants—who felt called by the Spirit to a radically new way of life. The monasticism they pioneered shaped the church for the next thousand years.

Abba Arsenius, a well-educated member of the upper class in Rome, left his promising career in the late fourth century to learn the wisdom of the desert in Egypt. Once a visitor asked him why he, who had studied the classics, would ask a poor Egyptian peasant for counsel. "I have indeed been taught Latin and Greek," Abba Arsenius said, "but I do not know even the alphabet of this peasant."[1]

Ideas are important, and we don't want to overlook the gifts of a formal education. But what was true in the fourth-century desert is true in our neighborhoods as well. We've learned a lot about prayer from people who've never read a book on prayer and wouldn't think of writing one. What they know, they've learned through years of praying. What they offer is an inheritance of spiritual wisdom.

I (Jonathan) am a member of the St. John's Baptist Church, a historically black congregation across the street from Rutba

House in Walltown. At St. John's, prayer is important. No one offers a course on prayer at our church, and I don't think the pastor has ever preached a sermon on the topic. But I have learned to pray in the Spirit there. I've learned by watching how Mother McCrea does it.

She starts by waiting. "We gonna pray now, children," she'll say, and she asks us to hold hands in a circle. With her head bowed and her eyes closed, Mother McCrea will start swaying back and forth. She might moan a little bit, but she doesn't say anything. Her body in a rhythmic motion, you can sense her spirit getting still. "Centering" is what a spiritual director might call it. At St. John's we call it "waiting on the Lord."

You never know just how long it's going to take, but at some point Mother McCrea will start whispering, "Thank You, Lord. Thank you, Jesus." And somebody else will say, "Thank you!" Together there in the presence of the Lord, aware of God's infinite goodness, all there is to say is, "Thank you."

As she repeats herself over and over, like an Eastern monk saying the Jesus Prayer, Mother McCrea will start to remember God's goodness down through every generation. "You've brought us a mighty long way," she'll shout, listing signs of God's faithfulness to Israel, to us. She takes us from Pharaoh's Egypt all the way up to the present—to the grace God has shown us today. "You woke us up this morning, started us on our way."

Then, immersed in God's presence, Mother McCrea will ask that we might draw nearer. "Fill us, Holy Spirit! Have your way, God. Move in this place!" We are immersed in the presence of the greatest power in the universe. And following Mother McCrea's lead, we are asking God to come closer. We are bouncing up and down, shouting as loud as we can, "Yes,

Lord! Please, Lord." We are begging with our whole bodies to live every moment in this presence.

But everyone in the room knows there are other powers present in the world. A brother at church who has been in that prayer circle longer than me (I'll call him Leroy) testified one Wednesday night about a struggle he'd had with a demon. Leroy was an addict for over twenty years of his life. He will tell you how Jesus set him free from crack cocaine, but you wouldn't have to know his story to see that *something* happened to him. He shines with joy.

This particular Wednesday night Leroy stood up during testimony time looking very serious. He said he wanted to tell us what had happened to him the night before. Sometime after midnight, Leroy was awakened by a pressure on his chest that felt just like someone lying on top of him. Not only was this person on him; whoever it was had his hands around Leroy's neck. He couldn't move, and he couldn't breathe. Leroy thought he was going to die.

But then something told him that it was a demon attacking him, and that he needed to call on the name of Jesus. With what little strength he had left in him, Leroy cried out "Jesus!" and heard something hit the wall on the other side of his bedroom. With the weight gone from on top of him, Leroy jumped out of bed and turned on the light, but couldn't see a thing.

By this point in the story, tears were streaming down Leroy's face and both of his hands were lifted in the air. "I just want to say, 'Thank you, Jesus!' " he cried out. Those of us gathered at St. John's that evening joined our brother in thanking God for the presence of the Holy Spirit and the power of Jesus' name to drive away the enemy.

Leroy didn't know that his story could have come straight out of Athanasius's *Life of Anthony*. He didn't need to. Trying to live his whole life in God's presence, our brother had come up against the same enemy that St. Anthony battled in the Egyptian desert. He had experienced the power of God to save and came to tell the rest of us about it.

One of our profs at Eastern University used to tell us that the same Holy Spirit that existed hundreds of years ago and did incredible miracles is still with us, in us and among us today. Do we believe that? We asked him why we didn't see many miracles today, and he replied, "We have created a way of life that does not need miracles. We get hungry and we go to the store and buy food. When we get sick, we go to the hospital. But people who have little, they still believe and rely on miracles to survive."

Visit this place, O Lord, and drive far from it all snares of the enemy; let your holy angels dwell with us to preserve us in peace; and let your blessing be upon us always; through Jesus Christ our Lord. Amen.

Book of Common Prayer

A friend of mine (Shane's) was working down in Latin America in a health clinic. They had very little supplies and one day ran out of everything except a bottle of Pepto-Bismol. So when people showed up with all sorts of illnesses, all they could offer them was Pepto. But my friend said, "The crazy thing is people were getting healed." They were coming with all sorts of illnesses and injuries, and the missionaries would give them Pepto-Bismol. And people were getting healed! A crowd of folks gathered from all over, and he said somehow that little bottle never ran out.

Our professor at Eastern went on to tell us that we should pray that we would become the sort of people who are safe for God to trust with miracles. We must become people who will not exploit or market

> *Lord, I believe; help thou mine unbelief.*
>
> **Mark 9:24** KJV

or pervert the power of the Spirit. We must become people who get out of the way of God.

Incomparably Great Power for Us Who Believe

As Paul is praying for the church to know our glorious inheritance in the saints, he starts talking like a Pentecostal preacher. He begs God to make plain for us the incomparably great power that is available to those who believe. He says this is the same power God used to raise Jesus from the dead. Then he insists that *this same power* is available to us. The greatest power in the universe—whatever you call the force that lifted Jesus from hell and put him high above every demon, every addiction, every *ism,* every kingdom, every worldly authority—*that* power is available to the church (Ephesians 1:20-21).

Ephesians says God has already given us a force more powerful than any enemy who might come against us. But the only way to access this power is to go deeper into God. The only way to learn our strength in Christ is to embrace Jesus in his weak human flesh.

If we really believe that the power of the Spirit lives in us, we will begin to shine—to experience the fire that St. Francis and the desert monastics knew so well. It will indeed consume us. When I (Shane) was in college, I spent a summer learning from Mother Teresa in Calcutta. One of the prayers I prayed every morning there was this:

Dear Jesus, help us to spread your fragrance everywhere we go.

Flood our souls with your spirit and life.

Penetrate and possess our whole being so utterly that our lives may only be a radiance of yours.

Shine through us, and be so in us, that every soul we come in contact with may feel your presence in our soul.

Let them look up and see no longer us but only Jesus!

Stay with us, and then we shall begin to shine as you shine; so to shine as to be a light to others; the light O Jesus, will be all from you, none of it will be ours; it will be you, shining on others through us.

Let us thus praise you in the way you love best by shining on those around us.

Let us preach you without preaching, not by words but by our example, by the catching force, the sympathetic influence of what we do.

The evident fullness of the love our hearts bear to you. Amen.

My (Shane) grandfather used to bale hay in the hills of East Tennessee. He was notoriously buying new tractors and equipment without my grandmother's consent. One summer he had just gotten a brand new truck and trailer, and wanted to "break 'em in." So he and my uncle began loading up the hay bales scattered across the field, higher and higher, pushing it to the limit.

Finally, when the trailer was loaded to the gills, they hit the road with the hay, my uncle driving and my grandfather rid-ing along proudly. What they didn't notice was that one of the hay bales was rubbing against the tire. Which is pure trouble, thanks to a little thing called friction.

Before long, the hay bale caught on fire, then another and another (it was hay, after all). Eventually, the truck looked like a comet headed down the highway. But my uncle and grandpa didn't notice. (They were probably talking about how nice the truck ran or jamming to the Chuckwagon Gang.)

People began to wave hysterically, and my uncle nodded back (that's how we roll in East Tennessee). But eventually, he looked in the mirror, saw the flames behind them, and quickly pulled over. This created new problems, as now the flames that had been behind them raged upward and began to melt the back of the truck.

My grandfather was in the glove compartment. My uncle asked what he was doing, and my grandfather pointed to the pile of stuff stacked on his jacket and said, "Well, I don't want this stuff to burn too."

But my uncle was not so quick to give in. He snapped back, "No, I've got an idea; get back in the truck." So they did. My uncle put the pedal to the metal and they hit the highway again, this time with the goal of "getting rid of the fire."

My uncle swerved the truck so the hay bales fell off behind them. Fields began to catch on fire. Fire trucks from all the neighboring counties were following them, putting out the damage, and they finally managed to extinguish the inferno. My grandfather told me, after he got out of jail (just kidding), "Shane, we caught half of East Tennessee on fire."

We used to laugh and laugh when Pawpaw told that story. But after some years of prayer in this kingdom adventure, I thought to myself, that is what the kingdom of God looks like. Christians blaze through this dark world and set it on fire with their love. It is contagious and spreads like wildfire. We are people who shine, who burn up the darkness of this old world with the Light that dwells within us. Maybe when we're dead and gone, people will look around and ask, "What in the world passed through here?"

We are not just called to be candles. Candles make for nice Christmas services and for a nice peace vigil (or a pretty Elton John song). They can remind us that God's light dwells within us, and that we are to shine that light amid this dark world. But we are not just called to be candles. We are called to be fire.

And when we say fire, we mean the kind of fire that purifies and cleanses, not the kind of fire that destroys. This is the gentle fire that the Scriptures speak of—the fire that melts away the impurities of precious metals. The fire that burns away the chaff and dead branches so that we may be more fully alive, as people and as a planet. The fire that consumes bushes and sinners without destroying them.

Candles can be snuffed out by the slightest wind or the smallest child on his or her birthday. But fire burns together. As we grow in spiritual wisdom, learning the dynamics of prayer, we are consumed more and more by the One who burns with love for the whole creation. We are to be fire, to weave our lives together so the Spirit's inferno of love spreads across the earth. Ultimately, that's what it means to become the answer to our prayers.

"If you are willing," Abba Joseph said, "you can become pure flame."

Epilogue

THIS BOOK HAS BEEN ABOUT the marriage of prayer and action. We began by suggesting that we need to pray like everything depends on God and live like God has no other plan but the church. We are the ones God is waiting on. When we throw our hands up at God and inquire, "Why do you allow this injustice!?" we have to be ready for God to toss the same question back to us.

Predictably, some will say it's absurd to assert that we are the answer to our prayers because God is the only answer to prayer. That's the beautiful mystery: *we have a God who chooses to need us.* We have a God who doesn't want to change the world without us. We have a God who longs to cooperate with us, to allow us to fail and flounder and who promises to make up for our shortcomings, but nonetheless *wants* us. It's the story of our faith. Certainly nothing hinges on our own ingenuity or strength; quite the opposite—God works through weakness.

This is the great paradox and humor of God's audacious power: a stuttering prophet will be the voice of God, a barren old lady will become the mother of a nation, a shepherd boy will become their king, and a homeless baby will lead them home. God works not in spite of but *through* our frailty.

Consider the miraculous feeding of the thousands we find in the Gospels. The conversation goes something like this. The disciples are concerned that the people are hungry and approach Jesus. Jesus' response is brilliant: "Well, give them something to eat!" The disciples are still thinking with the mind of the market economy and cannot possibly conceive of how to hit up the local Wal-Mart and feed all these people. "That would take eight month's wages!" How in the world could they possibly afford to feed these people?

Jesus' response (again, characteristically brilliant) is to ask them: "What do you have?" All they have is a meager offering of a little kid's sack lunch—some fish and chips. But he is willing to give everything he has. So Jesus takes it and adds a little Godstuff.

He proceeds to take the meager offerings of a little kid's lunch to feed the entire crowd of thousands. And when all is said and done, there are leftovers. The unmistakable lesson is that God will take whatever we have if we offer it with open hands and a willing heart—and God will use it to work miracles, feed thousands, change the world.

So when we see a problem like the starving masses, is the answer God or is the answer us? We think Jesus would answer YES. The answer is *both*.

Now, we shouldn't ever think that we are God, or that we are the hope of the world or the ones who move history. That's what is so dangerous about the theology of empires and kings and presidents and maybe even some well-intentioned rock stars. We can begin to think we are the ones who move history or have the power to change the world.

But God lives in us and through us. In fact, Scripture even says, "No one has ever seen God; but if we love one another, God lives in us" (1 John 4:12). You are the only Jesus some people will ever see. We get to become the body of Christ, to be people who remind the world of Jesus. We are God's body. None of us is Christ alone, but all of us are Christ together. We are God's body in this world.

Even as God lives in us, God is also bigger than us. So when we fall short, grow tired or lose hope, God is still there, resurrecting broken dreams, healing broken hearts, restoring a broken world. Let us never begin to think we are the answer *without God*.

Perhaps no one understood the need to pray *and* to act better than the historic black church in the fight against slavery. We can hear in the words of the old spirituals an utter dependence on God, the groaning of a people for a Deliverer, for someone to take them home and save them from this terrible injustice. And we can also hear in their words a dream for a better world and see in their actions the enactment of that world.

Author and historian Tonya Bolden captures a dynamic encounter between Sojourner Truth and Frederick Douglass.[1] Shortly after the passage of the Fugitive Slave Act in 1850 that required that runaway slaves be brought back to their masters, Frederick expressed his despair to Sojourner. Slavery seemed so permanent. The problems seemed insurmountable. He was losing hope that they could ever end slavery. Sojourner chastised his lack of faith with four little words: "Frederick, is God dead?"

Those words appear on her gravestone as a sign not of her doubt but of her deep faith in a God who can change the world if we will only use our lives to join God's dream and to interrupt everything that stands in the way.

So let us pray. And let us become God's answer to our prayers.

Notes

Chapter 1: An Invitation to Beloved Community
[1]While God is Father, many women in our communities and in the church have helped us learn about the feminine images of God in Scripture. This is important—not only because God is not an old man on a throne in the sky but also because we miss a lot of the good things about God if we only recognize the divine attributes that seem "masculine." One helpful book is Paul R. Smith's *Is It Okay to Call God "Mother"? Considering the Feminine Face of God* (Peabody, Mass.: Hendrickson, 1993).

Chapter 2: Begging for God's Economy
[1]See the Relational Tithe website at www.relationaltithe.com.

Chapter 3: Temptations Along the Way
[1]Concert in Lufkin, Texas, on July 19, 1997.

Chapter 5: Praying as a Peculiar People
[1]Maltbie D. Babcock, "This Is My Father's World" (1901).
[2]Rodney Clapp, *A Peculiar People* (Downers Grove, Ill.: InterVarsity Press, 1996), pp. 154-57.
[3]See the Christian Healthcare Ministries website at www.chministries.org.
[4]Rodney Stark, *The Rise of Christianity* (Princeton, N.J.: Princeton University Press, 1996), p. 98.
[5]In his book *The New Friars* (Downers Grove, Ill.: InterVarsity Press, 2006),

Scott Bessenecker has provided a good introduction to the theology and practice of these new missions organizations. For a more in-depth look at life in these communities, see John B. Hayes, *Sub-merge: Living Deep in a Shallow World* (Ventura, Calif.: Regal Books, 2006). Also see Christopher L. Heuertz, *Simple Spirituality: Learning to See God in a Broken World* (Downers Grove, Ill.: InterVarsity Press, 2008).
[6]For the twelve marks of new monasticism, see www.newmonasticism .org.

Chapter 6: Growing Deeper in Spiritual Wisdom
[1]*The Sayings of the Desert Fathers: The Alphabetical Collection 1,* trans. Benedicta Ward (Kalamazoo, Mich.: Cistercian Publications, 1975), p. 103.
[2]Gregory of Nyssa, *The Life of Moses,* trans. Abraham J. Malherbe and Everett Ferguson, Classics of Western Spirituality, Cistercian Studies 31 (New York: Paulist Press, 1978), pp. 21-22.

Chapter 7: Receiving Our Inheritance
[1]*The Sayings of the Desert Fathers: The Alphabetical Collection 1,* trans. Benedicta Ward (Kalamazoo, Mich.: Cistercian Publications, 1975), p. 10.

Epilogue
[1]Tonya Bolden, *The Book of African-American Women: 150 Crusaders, Creators, and Uplifters* (Holbrook, N.J.: Adams, 1996).

About the Authors
(and Their Communities)

Shane Claiborne is an author, activist and recovering sinner—a Tennessee hillbilly with a love for Bluegrass. He is a founder of The Simple Way (www.thesimpleway.org) and a long-term partner in the Potter Street Community, an intentional community in Kensington, Philadelphia. He is a board member of the Christian Community Development Association, whose pillars are reconciliation, redistribution and relocation. Shane has helped birth and connect radical faith communities and intentional hospitality houses. He's also a little rusty on his circus skills but has been known to do a little juggling and fire-breathing on occasion.

Jonathan Wilson-Hartgrove lives with his wife, Leah, their son, JaiMichael, and other friends at the Rutba House in Durham, North Carolina. He is associate minister at the historically black St. John's Baptist Church and directs the School

for Conversion, a migratory program for theological education and formation in Christianity as a way of life (www.new
monasticism.org). Jonathan is the author of *Free to Be Bound:
Church Beyond the Color Line* (NavPress) and *New Monasticism: What It Has to Say to Today's Church* (Brazos Press).

The Simple Way and **Rutba House** communities are part of
a larger network of communities, sometimes referred to as
a "new monasticism." They're quietly trying to pray and live
the kingdom in cities and towns throughout North America.
For more information about communities near you, visit www
.communityofcommunities.us.

LIKEWISE. *Go and do.*

A man comes across an ancient enemy, beaten and left for dead. He lifts the wounded man onto the back of a donkey and takes him to an inn to tend to the man's recovery. Jesus tells this story and instructs those who are listening to "go and do likewise."

Likewise books explore a compassionate, active faith lived out in real time. When we're skeptical about the status quo, Likewise books challenge us to create culture responsibly. When we're confused about who we are and what we're supposed to be doing, Likewise books help us listen for God's voice. When we're discouraged by the troubled world we've inherited, Likewise books encourage us to hold onto hope.

In this life we will face challenges that demand our response. Likewise books face those challenges with us so we can act on faith.

likewisebooks.com